THE

100

Greatest Ideas for Making Money on the Internet

Ros Jay

WH
S

THE

100

Greatest Ideas for Making Money on the Internet

Ros Jay

CAPSTONE

The right of Ros Jay to be identified as the author of this work has been asserted in accordance with the Copyright, Designs and Patents Act 1988

First published 2000 by
Capstone Publishing Limited
Oxford Centre for Innovation
Mill Street
Oxford OX2 0JX
United Kingdom
http://www.capstone.co.uk

British Library Cataloguing in Publication Data
A CIP catalogue record for this book is available from the British Library

ISBN 1-84112-102-9

Typeset in 11/14 pt Plantin by
Sparks Computer Solutions Ltd, Oxford
http://www.sparks.co.uk
Printed and bound by
T.J. International Ltd, Padstow, Cornwall

This book is printed on acid-free paper

Substantial discounts on bulk quantities of Capstone books are available to corporations, professional associations and other organisations. For details telephone Capstone Publishing on (+44-1865-798623) or fax (+44-1865-240941).

Contents

Eight Greatest Ideas for Giving Better E-service 27

Seven Greatest Ideas for Expanding your Business on the Internet 31

Eleven Greatest Ideas for Promoting your Internet Business 47

Five Greatest Ideas for Starting Up and Selling an Internet Business   *61*

Six Greatest Ideas for Choosing an Internet Business   *73*

Nine Greatest Ideas for Making Money Without Even Starting a Business

Eight Greatest Ideas for Small Businesses on the Internet

Eleven Greatest Ideas for
Designing a Profitable Web Site   105

Four Greatest Ideas for
Making Money on the Stock Market   117

Two Greatest Ideas for Billing over the Internet   123

*I*ntroduction

Surely everyone must have got the message by now? The Internet has arrived and will change forever the way we make money, in business or out of it. The people who predicted it would never catch on – who said it was the emperor's new clothes – are being proved wrong every day. Like most technologies, the Internet needs to reach a critical mass before the floodgates really open. Remember when fax machines (that creaky old technology) first appeared? Plenty of companies held out for a couple of years before buying them, but their use climbed to the point where everyone just couldn't manage without one, and suddenly ... everyone had one. The Internet is right on the brink of doing the same thing.

Most businesses are online already, of course, and most are happily using email technology. But this isn't even the tip of the iceberg in terms of recognising the potential of the World Wide Web. Many people point at the new Internet millionaires and say, 'They may be worth £400 million, but look, their business only made £100,000 profit last year.' This is missing the point.

The point is not what the business made last year, but what it will make next year and the year after. The City experts can't all be wrong. If they reckon a business is worth £400 million, who are we to say they're out by a few thousand per cent? Isn't it more likely that they recognise the real potential of the Net? We would be far better off joining in the gold rush than standing back and watching sceptically until we're proved wrong.

Prepare for take-off

So when is the Internet finally going to take off and fly? The prediction is that it will happen soon – very soon. At the moment, there are 12 million Internet users in the UK; a figure which is forecast to more than double by 2004. But it is not only the numbers that are important; it is people's familiarity with the Net.

There was a time when mail-order businesses were hard to make a success of. People didn't like putting money in the post; they preferred to walk into a shop and hand over the notes, and walk out with the goods under their arm. And yet mail order is now a huge industry, and more and more people are finding they are quite happy to buy long distance. One of the often-quoted problems with the Net is that plenty of people surf it, but relatively few are happy to spend money online. But this will change too, for all sorts of reasons:

- As people start to try it they will find it is perfectly reliable, so long as they stick with trustworthy businesses, just as you have to when you buy mail order or at a car boot sale, or even at a high street shop.
- A growing number of products and services will be available only online. A good example of this is lastminute.com (see *Idea 93*). If you want to book a cut-price, last-minute flight or hotel room, they have offers you won't find anywhere else.
- Buying online gives you access to overseas goods which you would never find offline. Some entail shipping problems, but many don't. It's easy to buy wine direct from France online, for example.
- Many online goods are much cheaper than the same goods offline. You can easily save 40 per cent, for example, if you buy a car online from Europe, instead of at the local UK dealership (see *Idea 93*).

In a sense, the promise of the Internet has already been fulfilled, at least for some. The Internet pornography market was the first to take off (see *Idea 50*), and is now generating serious money unlike any other industry. In fact, the porn industry is pioneering much of the new technology on the Net, and is way ahead of almost anyone else. It proves that, once customers catch on to the benefits of the Web, businesses boom.

So who's making money on the Internet?

The fact that you've picked up this book indicates that you recognise the Net's potential. We hear enough stories about Internet millionaires – who are these people, how do they do it, and how can we get a slice of the same pie? We know there are fortunes to be made in cyberspace – how can we make sure that we are the ones who make them?

The good news is that just about anyone can make money out of the new technology. There isn't a single type that succeeds. There are huge organisations on the Net, bringing in a huge amount of traffic to their sites, for example, through well-placed advertising (see *Idea 32*). There are the big Internet companies themselves, too, such as Yahoo and Netscape, many of whom started out in the early days of the Internet by giving away free listings or free software to attract visitors. Most of them make much of their money through selling advertising (see *Idea 49*).

Then there are smaller businesses, who may exist exclusively on the Web, or who may be adding an Internet arm to their existing business. These businesses range from the experienced to those run by groups of young, inexperienced people who have little beyond a great idea, plenty of good sense and a lot of dedication (for example, see *Idea 51*).

And that is one of the most exciting things about the Net: you don't have to be a middle-aged middle manager to make a fortune (although plenty of middle-aged middle managers have found a new lease of life in Internet businesses). In fact, you don't even have to have a business at all, as you'll see in *Ideas 54–62*. Come to that, you don't have to make a fortune either – there are plenty of ways of adding a modest sum to your income without much effort, or even ways of saving money – from a few pounds to a few thousand pounds (*Ideas 89–96*).

Be a fast learner

When a new industry starts up, it generates a whole set of new rules for succeeding in business. We all know the key rules of selling by now, or the key ways to make a direct mailshot effective. And if we don't know, we just pay someone else to tell us. But what are the basic rules for designing an effective Web site (*Ideas 71–81*)? Or the guidelines for successful e-service strategy (*Ideas 9–16*)? What are the key ways of promoting an Internet business (*Ideas 32–42*)?

These guidelines do exist; enough businesses have tried and, by their success or failure, found out what works. But the word hasn't really got around yet. That's why so many businesses are getting it so horribly wrong. They are often the ones who say that the Internet doesn't work. But in fact, it doesn't work for them. That doesn't mean it can't work for you. Because you have access to something they haven't yet learnt: the hundred greatest ways to make money on the Internet. Go make a million.

*E*ight *G*reatest *I*deas for *E*-commerce

There are all sorts of nifty ideas for using the Internet to deal in shares (*Ideas 82–85*) or get paid for picking up your emails (*Idea 55*), as well as going all out for making a fortune by selling your Internet business. But actually, for most businesses, plain old-fashioned selling is still just about the best way to make money.

But although, in essence, selling is always selling, you do have to play the game a little differently on the Internet. The priorities are different, and your customers' and prospects' attitudes to your Web site may not be the same as their attitudes to your organisation offline.

For a start, you need to attract visitors to your Web site before you can sell them anything. And once you've got them there, you have to persuade them to stay. So you'll find plenty of ideas here for doing both. I'm not going into Web site design here because we'll look at that later; we're concentrating on strategy here.

Idea 1 – Know the Internet shopper

Targeting is at the heart of any marketing campaign. If you want to attract business over the Net, you need to target your efforts at the people who are out there using it and spending money online. The most successful Internet businesses when the Web first took off were largely the ones selling software and Internet-related products and services. That was because just about everyone who was online was in the market for such goods – they were all computer nerds.

Things have broadened out a lot since then. But there are still certain types of people who are far more likely to be online than others. And of those, a narrower band who are likely to spend money over the Web. So who are they?

- Internet users are mostly male, well educated, and the average age is around 35. However, people who *buy* over the Net are as likely to be female as male.
- Internet shoppers are on average older than non-shoppers.
- Internet shoppers also have higher incomes than non-shoppers.

As far as attitudes to products are concerned, people who spend money online tend to:

- want convenience;
- be more impulsive than non-buyers;
- be looking for variety;
- be innovative;
- be less averse to risk than non-shoppers; and
- be less concerned with price and brand than Internet users who don't buy.

If you're starting up an Internet business, you'll obviously want to sell something that the typical Internet shopper might want to buy. If you have an existing business, you can still take this profile into account when you develop products and services for sale over the Internet. For example, promotions can work well on the Net because Internet shoppers are more impulsive buyers. They are also looking for variety and for convenience, so try to offer these whatever you are selling. And focus on giving detailed information rather than worrying about giving the best deal. Quality is more important than price.

Idea 2 – Start with what you know

When businesses start getting excited about being on the World Wide Web, they immediately begin to think about all the new possibilities out there, all the potential customers who have never even heard of them yet. Until now ... Just imagine all the new business they'll attract with their beautiful new Web site.

But wait. Who is actually going to visit your Web site? The evidence shows that you are far more likely to be visited by existing customers than prospective ones. And that existing customers are far more likely to order from you online when they do visit. In fact, existing customers are an all round good thing; they are also more likely to have a positive attitude to your Web site, and put up with flaws and imperfections in it for longer.

So the idea here is that you should keep your existing customers very much in mind when you design and run a Web site. They are the ones who matter. And if they check out your Web site and find that it doesn't do what they want it to, they will take away a bad feeling which will impinge on their offline dealings with you as well.

So what do your customers want from your Web site? Obviously you will need to ask them, either on or offline. But they are likely to want a shortcut to order products without having to browse them first – they already know what they buy from you. They may well want the facility to track orders. And they may also want a secure method of checking their order history with you.

American Airlines is often held up as an example of a great Web site (www.aa.com). When they launched it in 1995, they had designed it specifically for their best customers – their AAdvantage frequent flyers. They knew, for example, what questions their customers most often asked them, and made sure they answered these on their Web site. And they made it possible for their customers to book their flights over the Web. They also listed flight schedules for their own airline and for their competitors'. They knew that many of their customers wouldn't book a flight until they had compared it with the competition, so they let them check it out without leaving the Web site.

American Airlines' strategy was hugely successful. Of course new prospects log on to the site regularly as well, and American now clocks up several million page views every week. It is the most popular airline site on the Net, and it all began by targeting the organisation's top customers.

Ask yourself

What do your customers want from your Web site that you're not giving them at the moment? What do they want from you offline that they might also want online? How can you find out?

Idea 3 – Search the Web

The amount of information available on the Web is mind-numbing, and it includes contact details for just about every person or business you could want to sell to. The only trouble is sifting out the tiny fraction that you want from the rest. But once you know how, using the Net to find business leads is a great idea.

There are three key ways to find new sales leads online: newsgroups, mailing lists and trade leads.

- *Newsgroups:* A number of newsgroups will accept postings. Try the following main groups: alt.business.import-export, alt.business.import-export.computer, alt.business.import-export.consumables, alt.business.import-export.food, alt.business.import-export.only, alt.business.import-export.raw-material, alt.business.import-export.services, and alt.business.import-export.offshore.
- *Mailing lists:* You can acquire mailing lists from various sites on the Web. If you want general directories you could try www.search.com. Also check out www.ciber.bus.msu.edu/ for a listing of other contacts.

- *Trade leads:* If you want to be kept posted of trade opportunities around the globe, you can get listings from www.ciber.bus.msu.edu/.

Idea 4 – SPAM, SPAM, SPAM and SPAM – without the SPAM

Direct selling – going direct to your customers and prospects – is an increasingly popular way of selling outside cyberspace. But for some reason we seem to have a more passive approach to the Internet. We expect customers to come to us, rather than the other way around. But why not try both ways?

Email campaigns are simply an electronic version of direct mail. And we all know that direct mail can be one of the most effective sales tools. However, email has a different etiquette from snail mail which you need to know before you launch a campaign. The most important thing to know is that unsolicited or untargeted email is a real no-no. It's known as spam, and it's considered totally out of order to send it. It is the electronic version of junk mail, but it generates a very different reaction.

If you send unsolicited mail through the post, most people tolerate it, and many welcome it and respond to it. But the psychology of email is different; spam almost invariably elicits a negative response, and often quite a hostile one. By the same token, you should never sell your emailing list without the co-operation of the people on it, even though it is legal to do so. Much better to give them a button to click on to indicate that they are happy for their name to be sold.

So how can you use email to make money on the Internet? Well, you can email existing customers, and anyone who has asked for you to send them information. Here are some ideas:

- Ask for an email address every time someone asks you for information, places an order or opens an account with you.

- Ask your customers and contacts if they would like to receive a regular email message containing product news or bargain deals.
- Launch an electronic customer magazine and ask customers if they would like you to email it to them each month. If it's useful enough, your contacts may be willing to subscribe to it.
- Offer your customers the option of receiving their messages as HTML-enhanced mail. This means you can send emails with graphics and layout, which can be far more persuasive than text-only emails. Show them a photo of the products on offer, or add animated headlines.
- Always make it easy – at every mailing – for your customers to remove themselves from your mailing list with a simple click of a button.

Email is much more personal than snail mail. We regard our own computers as extensions of ourselves, so emailing someone is much more intimate than sending them a letter. This explains why people resent unsolicited email so much, but it also means that email, when it is welcome, has far more impact than mail which drops through the letterbox.

Ask yourself

What snail mail do you currently send your customers which you could be sending by email instead?

Idea 5 – Building a brand

A brand is not just a name; it's a whole image. With a single word, your brand name should conjure up a whole assembly of visual associations in the minds of your customers and prospects. Rolls-Royce isn't just a name; it gives you a mental picture of the kind of people who drive their cars, the sort of lifestyle they lead and so on. A really effective brand name makes your prospects think not just 'I want that product', but 'I want to be the kind of person who buys that product.'

Generating a successful brand on the Web is particularly hard. In the outside world, you help to consolidate your brand image with the building you are based in, the staff who deal with customers, the way you all dress and so on. Your range of brand-building tools is much more limited on the Web.

On the other hand, branding is especially important in cyberspace. An effective brand will make your prospects and customers think of you first when they want to deal online – an essential factor with all that competition. To give you an example: where do you go when you want to order a book online? Almost certainly to amazon.com. They're the first online bookseller you think of. Imagine trying to survive on the Internet as a bookstore with Amazon as your competition.

The general rule with online branding is that the first business in any field to arrive on the Net has the best branding opportunity. The second has a tougher time, the third even tougher and so on. So if you arrive in an already busy market, branding is as difficult as it is crucial.

If you already have a successful offline brand, this is obviously a big help. But you still can't rest on your laurels. It is not so much your products or services which your brand image relies on, but the customer's experience at your Web site. If the technology lets them down, or the site is difficult to navigate, or your response is slow, your brand image will suffer.

So how can you build a successful brand online?

- Use a domain name that people can remember.
- Promote your Internet brand name offline, through PR and advertising.
- Try to provide something which the competition doesn't, such as useful industry information, better service or lower prices.

- Keep reinforcing your brand name with email campaigns (*Idea 4*), a bulletin board where users can contact each other, an ezine (electronic magazine), or other services which generate frequent contact.
- Follow the ideas for designing a profitable Web site (*Ideas 71–81*).
- Offer fast delivery of goods.
- Offer plenty of different order methods – phone, fax and snail mail as well as online.
- Make sure all your offline personnel know about your Web site and can talk helpfully about it to customers.

One of the key things Internet users look for in a brand is reliability. They need to trust you to buy from you online. So promote a trustworthy image:

- Show your physical contact details on your Web site.
- Give guarantees on your goods.
- Show testimonials and good reviews to build credibility.

Ask yourself

Which Internet brand do users instinctively think of first in your industry? What can you do to encourage them to think of you first?

Idea 6 – Get it together

All too many companies seem to think that their Web site is not connected to the rest of the business. It is often managed separately, and there is little co-ordination between online and offline activities. This is a great shame, because online and offline marketing can both boost each other's sales.

Suppose you see a magazine ad for a special promotion from a company you often do business with. You decide to check it out online. But when you log on to their Web site, you can find no mention of it. This will almost certainly irritate you, and may well put you off following up the promotion altogether. But are you sure you never do the same thing to your own customers?

Your marketing activities should be fully integrated, with one person in active charge of both offline and online advertising and promotion. Once you've got it together, you can start using your Web site to promote instore offers, direct mail to promote an online information directory, and any other ideas you have for attracting customers across the online-offline divide.

> *If one has not made a reasonable profit, one has made a mistake.*
>
> Li Xiannian

Here's the twist

You may have to tweak your management structure to achieve effective cross-departmental marketing. The people with direct responsibility for each area, traditional and Internet marketing, should all attend every marketing strategy meeting to be sure that they are working in tandem.

Idea 7 – Hi! I'm Nettie, your virtual shop assistant. How can I help you?

If a customer calls your sales office or walks into one of your stores, you rely on your sales staff to smile, be helpful, and guide the shopper through your products to help them find the right one for them. They may have all sorts of questions they want to ask, or need advice on the sort of product they need. Not only that, but a good salesperson will also make the customer welcome, and give them that warm, fuzzy feeling that makes them feel looked after.

But you don't get all that on the Net. You log onto an impersonal site and you have to find your own way round, with the help of what amounts to little more than a map with a few guidelines attached.

Not any more. The latest idea to arrive on the Web is the virtual shop assistant. This piece of software has been developed to counteract the current self-service style of Internet shopping, which many customers feel is less friendly and personal than picking up the phone or walking into a shop.

A virtual shop assistant combines all the best attributes of your real sales assistants, to give your Web site visitors the sense that they are being guided personally around your product range just as they would be offline. They are met by their virtual assistant when they log on, with a photograph and a greeting. What then follows is in effect a flow chart of questions with click-box answers. But it is packaged in such a way as to give the impression that you are being guided by your sales assistant rather than finding your own way around. And, just like any good sales assistant, your virtual assistant eases you gently from browsing to buying in a such a way that you barely notice.

The virtual shop assistant is a terrific idea for giving personal service – or at least the impression of it – on your Web site. If you want to see an example, try www.cozone.com, who have a range of assistants so realistic that, despite being mere pieces of software, they actually receive personal email from appreciative cozone.com's shoppers. What's more, they have had a considerable impact on sales.

Idea 8 – Why should you do all the work?

Have you ever placed an order online only to be sent an email confirmation of your order within the next half hour? And wouldn't you like to be able to do the same for your customers? What you need is a robot – an automatic response robot. This isn't an employee made of metal; it's a program which responds automatically to emails, orders or requests from your Web site visitors.

Automation is essential if you're operating a busy Web site. You can't possibly spare the personnel to send regular promotional emails to customers, mail out brochures, confirm orders and so on. And yet these are all vital services. It is this sort of fast response which will ensure that your customers enjoy doing business with you.

Automated follow-up to information requests can have a huge impact on sales, too. Experts reckon that prospects need to see your product promoted an average of seven times before they buy from you. An automatic response robot can follow up every request with a personalised email, and a further one if they haven't bitten yet, and can continue to send out as many emails as you want it to. So your prospects get all the reminders they need, and you don't have to do anything.

Automation programs can do all sorts of clever things. They can mail out regular newsletters and bulk emailings, and they can respond to emails from customers. The way they respond is by looking for keywords which you program; for example, you program your robot to recognise the word 'remove' and to remove the sender from your mailing list.

Here's the twist

It can be a problem if someone sends you a specific request by email, since no one actually reads your emails for you. If your robot doesn't understand the email, it can't respond correctly. There are two standard solutions here:

1 Program your robot to recognise and handle certain requests, and to forward all other email to your mailbox so you can deal with it.
2 Have two email addresses and ask Web site users to use one of them for certain specified communications such as brochure requests, and to use the other for all other enquiries.

Eight Greatest Ideas for E-service Strategy

When you sell over the Internet your customers can't see you and they can't hear you. They can't even see the building you operate from. And they may never communicate directly with a real person. So you have to work extremely hard to persuade them that they want to do business with someone they have never spoken to, heard or seen.

E-service is the key. You need to bend over backwards to make them feel welcome and wanted, and to show that even without direct communication you are operating a system which can still supply everything they could want, from their own order history to gift wrapping.

Many of your Internet customers will follow the profile I've just described. But many of them will also contact you offline. When they do, they will regard online and offline contact as being two sides of the same coin. Many businesses, unfortunately, seem to have little or no integration between these arms of the business.

If a customer writes to you and then follows up with a phone call, it shouldn't be a problem to put them through to someone who has a record of the letter. If they order online and then phone you, it should be equally easy to put them through to someone who has a record of their order. But is it? For too many companies, the operations are totally separate. So *Ideas 9, 10 and 11* are all about integration; the first step to successful e-service strategy.

Once you have integrated your service functions, you can go one step further for your customers and set up closed-circuit online communications between you and them (*Idea 12*) and make their visit to you more personal. The final ideas in this section will prevent the frustrating customer experience of not knowing whether the items they've ordered are in stock or, worse still, not being able to place an order at all.

Idea 9 – Integrate ... your dealings with your customers

One of the biggest buzz phrases in e-service at the moment is *customer relationship management*, or CRM. A CRM system is a computer-based system which manages your relationship with your customers – pretty much what you'd expect from the name really – so that you can access all the data you want on any customer at a single view from anywhere that you interface with them.

In fact, the phrase is frequently misused to describe a system that manages a single channel such as field sales management or promotions. A true CRM system embraces all channels of customer communication so that activities can be co-ordinated. This is as important in Internet dealings with customers as anywhere else, whether your Web site gathers leads, takes orders or run promotions. In many companies, especially in Europe (the US is somewhat further ahead), there simply isn't a strategy for responding to data collected over the Net. Companies may have an automated system for replying to brochure requests, but they don't feed in data on promotion responses, for example, to a central system.

The word is that CRM software and services are going to be in high demand over the next few years. Although CRM covers the whole gamut of customer-related activities, it is e-commerce that is driving its rapid growth. For one thing, the Internet has given customers the idea that things can happen fast; and fast responses demand integrated systems. Customers want to know on the spot whether you can deliver tomorrow; they want to be able to change an order online before you despatch it; they want a telephone reply to their email today. For another thing, the Internet makes all your competitors far more accessible to your customers and prospects, so the competitive edge needs to be that much sharper.

Installing a fully integrated CRM system is a terrific idea, but it is only the beginning. The investment is high – although it is increasingly essential anyway – so you'd better make the most of it. A surprisingly high number of CRM systems fail, in the eyes of the companies who invest in them. According to some surveys, the failure rate is as high as 75 per cent.

Why? Well, businesses are too inclined to install a system and then sit back and watch for it to show results. But the system has to be operated and exploited. It's important to make sure you install an adequate system, of course, but you also have to milk the system for all the value you can get out of it. Make sure everyone, from production and distribution to marketing and sales, are getting the most from it. And make sure you use it to deliver still better service to your customers, on the Internet and off it.

Ask yourself

What could we do for our Internet customers with a fully integrated CRM that we can't do at the moment?

Idea 10 – Integrate ... your call centres

More and more businesses are setting up call centres to offer customer support. What most of them are not doing is integrating this call centre with their Web site. But this is the essential next step for providing top-quality e-service. If your Web site visitors cannot access the information they want on the Web site, give them the option of calling you.

Most integrated systems operate by giving Internet customers a button to click which either puts a call through to a call centre or requests that they be called back on a number they key in (using a separate line if they have one). They are then connected within seconds to a call centre, and can speak to a real person. What's more, this real person can see on their screen exactly what information the caller has so far collected from the Web site.

This kind of system ignores the misconception that Internet customers want to deal with you only over the Web. They generally want the most convenient approach. Initially, this might seem to be the Net but, when they discover that they do need to speak to someone, an integrated system enables them to do so without delay or hassle.

Here's the twist

Integrating your call centre with your Web site entails integrating your queueing systems, too. You need to have a single queueing system for all your customers, whether they are accessing you via the phone, email or your Web site.

Idea 11 – Integrate ... your call centre with your data warehouse

Ok, so you've integrated your call centre with your Web site. Well done. But the next step in fully integrated CRM is to integrate your call centre with your data warehouse. The data warehouse is your store of information about all your customers, which should include their transaction details, address and personal details, financial data and profiling. By analysing this data you can predict trends, target campaigns and build profiles of future customers.

The data warehouse relies on the information that is fed into it from the operational end of your business. If the call centre isn't feeding in the data regularly, it becomes impossible to react swiftly to market changes. All data – whether it is acquired online or offline – must be fed into the data warehouse promptly to enable trends to be identified and analysed in terms of responsiveness, loyalty, risk and so on.

The reason you should integrate your call centre and your data warehouse is so that they can interreact to cut down your response times to market changes, and to monitor the effectiveness of marketing campaigns. For example, suppose you launch a particular promotion and you want to know if it's working, which type of customers are responding, and so on. An integrated system will enable your data warehouse to analyse this information quickly so that you can adapt the campaign as it proceeds. You might, for example, target the next wave of the campaign more accurately.

With business information and sales coming in online as well as by phone, fax and snail mail, it is essential to install a system that integrates fully with back-end functions.

Here's the twist

Many companies selling CRM systems would have you believe that what you need is a single-system customer database which takes in all marketing channels from your Web site to direct mail. But don't fall for this. It will never give you the sophisticated data analysis of a dedicated data warehouse. It is also less flexible in the long run than keeping your systems separate, and if the system goes down you lose everything.

Idea 12 – This feels like home

Personalisation is critical to build customer loyalty. It's essential that you find some way to make your customers feel as if they are getting a service that is unique to them. So why not give them a unique service? Why not give them their own home page? Instead of entering your Web site on your standard home page, you can invest in software that allows customers to create their own home page.

This makes a lot of sense psychologically. Once people invest something of themselves in your Web site, they become far more loyal to it and keener to keep returning. One of the best examples of this is www.tripod.com. Tripod is a Web community of young people not long out of full time education. It is an online magazine with articles on topics relevant to 18–34 year olds and which aren't taught in schools – anything from buying insurance to meeting new people. But it is far more than a magazine, with chats and discussion groups and a whole community feel to it.

Tripod started encouraging users to set up their own home pages, with huge success. Around 2500 people a day create a home page at Tripod. The Web site is so successful that in 1998 it was sold for $58 million. It was well worth it – a site with a million members, mostly in the lucrative 18–34 age bracket.

Idea 13 – Just between ourselves

Why would regular customers want to visit your home page every single time they enter your Web site? They probably don't want to at all, if they think about it. So don't make them do it. You can set up an extranet, which they can enter direct instead.

And what's an extranet? It's like an intranet but different. An intranet is an internal company Web site which is secure so that it can contain private information. An extranet is a closed-circuit Web site which you set up between you and your customer. You can link it to the rest of your Web site so that they can browse the whole site from it, but the extranet can contain an inventory of the products they have, details of new products which they might be interested in, special promotions and so on. It's more than just an order history, but it enables the customer to bypass your home page in favour of a personalised page.

Idea 14 – Keep checking your stock

Stock control isn't easy on the Internet. It is standard to allow customers to put items in their shopping basket and leave them there until they come back later and place the order. They may return in an hour, a week, or not at all. Most programs will tell customers when they select the item whether it is in stock or not. But what if they leave it in their shopping basket for a fortnight – can you promise them it's still in stock when they return?

You can't keep reserving items just because someone has put them in a shopping basket – you'd tie up far too much stock that way with no guarantee the purchase will even go ahead. So here's a better idea. Use a cookie (*Ideas 26* and *80*) to track when a customer places an item in a shopping basket. Then, if the customer goes offline, you can check on their return that the item is still available, and let them know. Meantime, you'll have some advance warning of a future leap in sales if you know that a number of possible orders are pending on a particular item. And check the stock once more when the customer finally orders, to make absolutely certain that the item is available for them.

Here's the twist

All this automation costs money, of course, but it is essential to invest in e-service if you want to get ahead of the field and stay there. If you don't do it, your competitors will. In fact they will anyway, so make sure you give priority to e-service.

Idea 15 – Any alternative?

Suppose a customer calls you on the phone to place an order for an item, which you don't have in stock. Do you say 'Sorry, we don't have it. Goodbye'? Of course you don't – at least I hope not. You offer them an alternative. 'I'm afraid we've sold out of it in dark blue, but we do have the light blue in your size.'

You can do this online too, although you may not have been lucky enough to experience it as a customer. But there certainly is software available which enables you to offer alternatives rather than disappoint customers.

Ask yourself

Are we losing sales online which we would have managed to make offline? What should we offer online to bring our service standards up to those we maintain offline?

Idea 16 – Don't go away ...

Has this ever happened to you? You visit a Web site, you like the look of the goods on offer, you try to place an order ... but it won't let you. There's a fault and there's nothing you can do. Order offline, come back later, or give up. Sometimes you can't even access the Web site because of some technical problem. Do you feel sympathetic? Not generally, no. You just feel irritated.

Are you sure this has never happened to your customers? *Idea 16* is all about preventing it happening to your customers. If your Web site is critical to your business, it's worth investing in a high-availability (HA) system. These, albeit expensive, systems basically contain two of everything so if any part of your site fails there is an automatic replacement.

Failing this, you could go for symmetric multiprocessing (SMP), which means that your site is served by multiple processors for different functions, such as database transactions or automated responses. If one processor goes down, the others simply take over. That has to be better than a 404 message.

Eight Greatest Ideas for Giving Better E-service

A good e-service strategy is essential, but it is the specific services you offer which customers will notice first, and the way that you offer them. Often the little touches will help your name stay in the visitor's mind rather than your competitors' names.

The ideas in this section are all little touches that can make a difference. You might be tempted to think that most of them are too insignificant to belong in a book on making money on the Internet. But if you thought that, you'd be wrong. Use all these ideas – and any others you can glean – to make the whole experience of visiting your Web site one that your customers wish to repeat … again and again. Now surely that has to be good for business.

Idea 17 – Get their details

Make sure that any enquiry response forms that you ask visitors to fill in include fields for their postal address and their phone number – otherwise you could easily lose them altogether. People change their email address much more frequently than their postal address.

Idea 18 – Follow up

Get this. A frightening proportion of companies don't even respond to enquiries made over the Internet. So *Idea 18* is simple – answer enquiries, and do it promptly.

Idea 19 – Sign here

Don't miss any opportunities with your outgoing emails. Make sure they are signed with a real person's name, and add contact details for them and for your organisation. You can also add your corporate slogan, or a brief promotion.

Idea 20 – Trust me, I'm a Web site

Trust building is essential with Internet customers. So when you ask them for personal data, tell them exactly why you want it and what you're going to do with it.

Idea 21 – Wrap it up nicely

Offer any little extras you can think of – at a reasonable charge – such as gift wrapping and gift cards.

Idea 22 – What's the magic word?

After someone places an order, put up an on-screen 'Thank you' message, instead of the ubiquitous, blunt 'Return to Shopping' button.

Idea 23 – Can you confirm that?

Send an email to confirm orders, along with another thank you. If this isn't an automated system (or even if it is) make sure this is prompt.

Idea 24 – I may only be an Internet customer, but I still exist

Treat your Web customers exactly the same way as your offline customers when it comes to after-sales support and service.

Ask yourself

What extras can we offer our customers and prospects online that will make them enjoy visiting our Web site even more?

Seven Greatest Ideas for Expanding your Business on the Internet

Once you have a Web site up and running, it shouldn't be simply another way of distributing your brochure or taking orders. An effective Internet presence is a way of increasing business in itself. If you are running a business exclusively online, it is your only way of growing.

You can expand your business by attracting more people to your Web site. The next section will look at advertising and promotion to do just that, but there are other ways too, as you'll find in *Ideas 25, 26, 27* and *28*. Some of these ideas, along with *Idea 29*, will also attract your existing customers to visit you more often.

And then there are ways to expand your business through other Internet sources, as you'll find in *Ideas 30* and *31*; both outsourcing and forming partnerships can give your business a boost, and are often far simpler to arrange on the Net.

So don't think that, just because you have a nice little Web site, you've done your job by giving customers the option of dealing with you online. You can set your horizons much wider than that.

Idea 25 – What was that address again?

Here's a simple but effective idea. A lot of browsers find your Web site by guessing the address. Maybe they wrote it down but they can't remember where they put it, or perhaps they already deal with you offline and have decided to try and find you online. But what if they guess wrong?

Suppose your Web site address is www.thebizness.co.uk. Anyone taking a shot in the dark might well try www.thebusiness.co.uk or www.thebizness.com, and they wouldn't be able to track you down. Unless you use web forwarding, that is. If you register any other domain names that you think prospects might try, you can make sure that they are automatically redirected to your Web site.

You can also use Web forwarding if your actual URL (Uniform Resource Locator) is hard to remember, or is a Web page provided by an ISP (Internet Service Provider) with an address that therefore seems less professional. Simply register and publicise a domain name you prefer, and then use Web forwarding to direct all visitors to your site. Web forwarding is also essential if you change your URL for any reason, to ensure that visitors are automatically redirected to your new location.

Ask yourself

Could we be losing customers because they are using the wrong Web site address?

Idea 26 – Ask the right questions

Visitors to your Web site will often give you information directly, perhaps because you ask for their details when they place an order or subscribe to a service. But there is other information to be gleaned less directly, which you don't want to miss out on.

All sorts of software products allow you to track and analyse the way your visitors behave. Perhaps the best known of these is the cookie (see also *Ideas 26* and *80*), which is simply a text file that identifies a particular visitor. It rests on their browser, and can be tracked by your server. The point of cookies is that they allow you to establish the preferences and habits of particular visitors, so that you can target them with the most promising advertising. (You can also use cookies for other functions, such as to enable repeat visitors to enter password protected sites easily.)

Other products log how visitors use your Web site, so you can find out, for example, which pages they visit and in what order. This sort of information log can build up a picture for you which will show up weaknesses in your site, such as which pages visitors tend to leave from, which discourage them from buying, or which items seem to be hard to find.

Analysing your server data is an excellent form of research, which will help you to make your Web site more appealing, and encourage people to stay for longer and to order more from you. But like all research, it is worthless unless you follow it up. So once you've installed the software, make sure you collate the data regularly and act on it. Redesign pages and routes through your site when you can see scope for improvement, and use the information gleaned from cookies to put targeted promotions in front of visitors.

Ask yourself

Are we missing opportunities simply by failing to collect information that is already there?

Idea 27 – Market research on the Net

Market information is vital, of course, for every part of your operation from product development to advertising and sales. But how do you acquire that market knowledge? Specifically, how do you research the people who visit your Web site?

It's quite straightforward to find out how many people visit your site, who they are, and what they do once they're there (see *Idea 26*). You can glean all this information without ever telling your site users that you're doing so. And it's extremely useful information, too. But it's far from being the whole story.

The thing is, while all of this information is useful, you're following the software products. You're learning whatever it is that your software is prepared or able to tell you. What you need next is to be able to write your own list of questions. For example, analysing your server data will tell you plenty, but it won't tell you *why* your customers visit you rather than the competition. It can tell you which pages they visit on your site, but it can't tell you what they were looking for and never found. If you want the answers to specific questions, you'll have to communicate directly with your Web site visitors. Ask them, in other words.

If you don't ask, you might never find out that no one orders certain products because you don't show photographs of them, or that what they really want is an order tracking facility, or that a lot of frustration would be saved if you displayed your delivery times more prominently. And market research can inform strategic decisions too. Your online customers might tell you that they favour you over the competition because your service is so much better... but the competition is catching up. Or that they aren't expecting to use your services for much longer because the trend is towards an alternative technology which you don't produce. So market research isn't an option – it's an essential survival tool.

So how do you go about doing market research on the Web? Well, there are two main types of research: qualitative and quantitative. Qualitative research is an open-ended form of research, in which you invite users to comment. The most effective methods on the Web are focus groups, usability testing and email feedback. Quantitative research is geared towards getting lots of simple answers (yes/no or tick box) to the same set of questions, using surveys and questionnaires. Let's start with qualitative research.

Qualitative research can be broken down into:

- focus groups;
- usability testing; and
- email feedback.

Focus groups

This simply entails getting a group of people – representatives of your Web site user base – together to discuss your Web site. In an ideal world, you would hire a moderator to run the group while you watch, the moderator being skilled at getting focus group members to talk constructively. However, you could just invite a few customers and prospects to join you for lunch and a discussion. Here are a few pointers:

- Write a list of questions or discussion points in advance.
- Have Web site access at the meeting, along with any other relevant materials such as designs for a new site or new pages and so on.
- Record the focus group meeting either on video or at least on audio tape.
- Don't give your own views, and try not to bias the questions. Your job is to remain objective.
- Make sure that the quieter members of the group have their say.

You can, of course, run a focus group online. This is done by inviting about six to twelve people to join a chat. Discussion isn't necessarily quite as smooth flowing as it is face-to-face, but the costs are low and you also have the bonus of an immediately available transcript.

Usability testing

Again, if you have the money you can pay a specialist organisation to test your Web site. But if you don't, you can organise it yourself. Simply find potential customers or visitors to your Web site, and ask them to come and test it for you. People never mind being asked, and it isn't hard to find willing volunteers. It is much better to use an existing customer than your best mate, because it's easier to be objective. And your best mate isn't necessarily in the market for the products or services you sell.

Usability testing should be done one-to-one, not in a group, and here are a few guidelines to follow:

- Don't guide the tester. The point of the exercise is to find out how easy the site is to use and navigate around under normal circumstances. And normal circumstances for most customers doesn't include having you standing over their shoulder. Just look to see what they have trouble with, what features they fail to notice, and so on.
- Make sure that during the course of the session the tester gets to check out most of the site – all of it if possible – even if this means moving them on at times. I know this doesn't appear to tally with the previous point, but the idea is to move them on if they get stuck in a rut or a loop, after first taking note of what was slowing them down.
- Let them check out the site in the order they choose. The more usability tests you do, the better idea you will get of patterns of usage. And people are different. Are you catering for the ones who like to start with a site map as well as those who prefer to start with a 'search the site' option?

Email feedback

You don't necessarily have to go out looking for this. Users will often email comments to you. But you can encourage this – and you should. Unsolicited email comments are not a reason to sigh deeply; they are exactly what you want. They are cost-free, hassle-free market research. So encourage people to email you with comments.

Emailed user comments are, however, expressions of strong views. No one's likely to mail you to say they thought your Web site was fine, and they quite liked being thanked for placing an order. Emails are for people who feel strongly enough to bother to send them.

One useful tip for email comments is to give users a simple feedback form instead of simply a blank page to fill up. Not only can you collect some useful quantitative data this way, you can also find out something about the person making the comment, which often helps you to interpret it better. If they are an IT manager, for example, their technical criticisms of your Web site will probably be useful, but not necessarily typical of your average user.

Don't make the form too long or your visitors will be fed up before they've completed it. For example, ask for name and job title or occupation, and contact details. Then ask one or two questions relating to your specific business or organisation. For example, if you run a cat fanciers Web site, ask emailers if they are an owner or a breeder, and of which breed of cat.

Quantitative research can be broken down into:

- site-centric research;
- product development;
- syndicated research; and
- panel research.

Site-centric research

It is notoriously difficult to get a handle on exactly who is out there in the cybermarket for your product – it often seems like a huge, nebulous mass of potential that you haven't a clue how to tap. But it ain't so hard really. The biggest clue you can get – or need – to who might buy from you is the people who already do so. If your current customers are all 30–40-year-old cycling enthusiasts with a high income, chances are that your most promising future prospects are going to be 30–40-year-old cycling enthusiasts with a high income. So the only question you need answered now is: who exactly are your existing customers?

This is where site-centric research comes in. Site-centric research is the process of gathering information by conducting surveys on your Web site. It is about the simplest and least expensive form of online research. Invite your site users to fill out a survey form online, in which you ask them the same kind of questions you would ask in an offline survey. For example:

- Find out about their experience of the Web – are they new to it or old hands? Have they visited your site before? This sort of information helps you decide how simple your site should be to navigate and what sort of features it should include.
- Ask for basic demographic information – age, gender and so on – to help you find the right tone and content for your site.
- Ask them to give you information about income, occupation and so on to help you with content and also to make your site more attractive to advertisers.

Most of the general rules for surveys apply here. For example, make it quick and easy to fill in; use yes/no and tick box replies so that you can collate the responses easily; ask the more personal questions (such as income details) at the end; use brackets for age and income type questions ('Do you earn below £10,000/£10,000–£19,999/£20,000–£29,999' etc). You can encourage people to respond to your survey by offering them some kind of incentive, such as a free gift or download, or money off their next online purchase.

The information you collect from site-centric research will be invaluable. By asking people how frequently they use your site, you can break the rest of the survey results down into groups of heavy, moderate and light users. You can then focus on targeting the heavy users – and others like them – on the basis that they will be the most profitable for your site.

You can also use this kind of research very effectively to survey your users' opinions of the site itself, particularly if you are planning an overhaul of the site.

Devise closed questions so you can collate the responses, and then include a box at the end for other comments.

Product development

This is a quantitative version of focus groups or usability testing. The answers may not be so in-depth, but they are more representative because you can use a much larger sample of users. Combining this with qualitative research gives you answers with both depth and breadth, of course.

With product development research, you simply invite your users to test a Web site that is in development, and then to answer a survey form about it. Again, you can offer them some kind of incentive about it. The most important thing with this kind of research is to be very clear about the questions you want answers to.

Syndicated research

Syndicated research means buying into nationally – or even internationally – conducted research. There are lots of questions which plenty of people want answers to, not just you. The costs vary according to the research you want to get your hands on, and they can be quite high, but they are an effective source of data on the national online buying habits of particular groups of people, which makes them one of the best sources of information about your market as a whole. If you sell cat toys, syndicated research will tell you how many cat owners there are in the country, what proportion of them are online, how much they spend on cat products and so on.

Panel research

Panel research, on or offline, involves contacting (traditionally by phone) a random sample of consumers and asking them all the same set of questions. So, for example, you might get interviewers to contact cat owners to find out how they feel about your products. But telephone panel research is extremely expensive, so research companies now operate online panel research.

They do this by building up vast databases of Web users who have agreed to be contacted, and have filled in a detailed questionnaire about their occupation, lifestyle, interests and so on. So they can select consumers to meet your profile very easily. The participants are offered incentives such as payments or prizes.

However ... Apart from the cost, which is not cheap, there is one other thing you need to know about panels. They are not always quite as random as they seem, because they are often recruited by inviting people to click on Web banners. Now, certain types of people are more likely to click on banners than others; the rate of ad-banner click-throughs is between only about one and two per cent. So these panels can be made up of people who are representative in many ways, but who belong to the small percentage of people who click on such banners. So, if you think this could introduce bias into the research, check with the research company how they recruit their participants.

The first step is to measure whatever can be easily measured. That is okay as far as it goes. The second step is to disregard that which can't be easily measured or to give it an arbitrary quantitative value. This is artificial and misleading. The third step is to presume that what can't be measured easily really isn't important. This is blindness. The fourth step is to say that what can't be easily measured really doesn't exist. This is suicide.

Robert McNamara

Idea 28 – Become an authority

A Web site magazine – or ezine – can be a great idea for attracting people to your site. In fact, its potential is so great that many successful online businesses are, in effect, nothing more than a highly popular ezine.

Mind you, I've seen far more ineffective ezines than effective ones. And if they don't work, they are simply a waste of resources. You need to launch a magazine that will genuinely attract visitors to your site. It's no good setting up a magazine just because everyone else is doing it.

So how do you start up a successful online magazine? Well, there are certain key rules you need to adhere to:

- *Have something to say.* This might sound obvious, but look at some of the stuff that's out there … You won't attract people to your site with a magazine that contains nothing new, nothing which they can't find elsewhere, and nothing which is interesting or useful. You have to offer something worth having. It might be the only comprehensive online listing of trade events in your industry, or interviews with really interesting authorities on your particular subject. You might include the only specialist classified advertising section for your industry or topic, or perhaps you carry important breaking news before anyone else.
- *Use original content.* Lots of people write articles and then try to sell them to ezines around the Web (wouldn't you, in their position?). But if you run these articles, you risk your visitors' feeling that you haven't got anything new to say; they've seen it all before on some other ezine. So make sure that your magazine carries as much original material as possible.
- *Update regularly.* An online magazine is not very different in essence from a mailed customer newsletter or magazine. But if you're going to use the electronic medium, it makes sense to exploit it. So what can you do in an online magazine that you can't do in an offline one? There are several answers to

this, of course, but one of the most useful things you can do is to update the ezine on a daily basis, at least in theory. This means that you can include breaking news, announcements, events listings and other items at short notice in a way that you can't do in print. So make the most of it.

- *Make it easy to navigate.* A printed magazine is easy to find your way around. You hold it in one hand and flick the pages with the other. But an online magazine is different. It needs a really clear and comprehensive contents page, plus a contents for each section. And you should include return options for both of these at the end of every page. You might also include options to go direct from any page to certain other popular pages without having to go via the main contents each time. And check out other good ezines for ideas, such as running a navigation bar with catchy article headlines down the side of each page, and links to related and archive articles.
- *Include archive material.* Here's something else you can do online but not in print. You can keep an archive of all past articles for people to browse or – if they have sufficient value – you can charge people to download them.
- *Make it fun.* Just because your ezine needs to be packed with stuff your visitors want to see, that doesn't mean it has to be serious. You can include all sorts of fun articles, pictures and even animation to entertain your readers. You might include the latest industry jokes, a horoscope, competitions, amusing stories, a humorous gossip column ... anything which will attract the kind of visitor you want. And that means keeping the design fun, too. Of course your interpretation of fun will vary depending on whether it is an ezine for merchant bankers or for ten-year-olds – but however important and serious the subject, people are still more likely to visit your site if the ezine is interesting or entertaining as well as useful.

If your ezine is sufficiently popular, you may be able to charge a subscription for it. This can be a nice little earner or it can, in some cases, be a serious money-spinner. And one of the great things about this idea is that, while it is great for attracting new business to established businesses, anyone operating out of a back bedroom at home can start a subscription ezine with nothing beyond a good idea which other people want information about.

Ask yourself

What information could you assemble into an ezine which would attract customers and prospects to your site? What information could you give them that no one else in the industry does?

Idea 29 – A sense of community

Online communities (OCs) are springing up all over the place. And it's not really surprising. There's a deep human need to belong to a community, and modern workstyles and lifestyles don't lend themselves to a community feeling. People who sit working at a computer terminal all day, very possibly at home or in the isolation of an office, want a sense of belonging to something.

There are OCs for most special interests, from bagpipe music to stamp collecting. And now, many businesses are creating a form of online community for their customers. Of course, just because someone is obliged to buy office stationery – or whatever you sell – it doesn't mean they are necessarily obsessed with the subject of comp slips. But there are many businesses whose customers or members have a real interest in their products or services.

One of the simplest and most effective ways to create this sense of community centred around your business is through a listserve. This is basically just a closed email list, whose membership you can control. You can use a listserve to email customers about promotions and new products (with their permission of course).

But you can go further than that. Email them regularly with items related to their area of interest, such as articles, tips, book reviews, jokes, interesting statistics – whatever they might want to know about. And put them in touch with each other.

The thing about a listserve (as opposed to a mailserve) is that everyone on it can mail everyone else, and the sender's name (rather than the list name) appears on the messages. Recipients can then choose to reply to the whole list or just to the sender. This means that your members or customers can start up their own discussions, and you can even supplement your listserve with realtime online chat (see *Idea 69*) and other services. Before you know it there's a whole community of doll's house collectors, or birdwatchers, or listed building owners or whatever it is … all focused around you.

Idea 30 – Why do it yourself when you can get someone else to do it for you?

Outsourcing is the increasingly popular practice of paying another organisation to take over tasks that you previously carried out in-house. So you might outsource your payroll management to another company, or the task of managing your car fleet. Outsourcing is different from standard contracting out, because you enter a long-term relationship with the company you outsource to, and work together closely with them. If you do decide to end the arrangement, you'll need a great deal of support from the supplier to hand over to their successor.

The reason businesses outsource is because the cost and demands of recruiting skilled personnel can be high, and outsourcing frees up valuable resources in terms of, for example, management time. Imagine how much more effectively you could run your business if you didn't have to worry about the payroll, fleet management, product design or whatever it is you outsource. If there are problems with staff off sick, computer failures, cash flow… well, they're not your problems anymore. You're paying someone else to worry about them.

You can outsource anything that isn't a core function that needs your strategic control. So long as a task is routine, easy to define and measurable, you can outsource it. So where does the Internet come into all this, you may be wondering?

The answer is that the Internet opens up all sorts of outsourcing opportunities because of the speed at which it operates. You can outsource the management of your accounts, for example, and download accounts data from your supplier at a moment's notice. Even order management and personnel information can now be outsourced, and data can flow back and forth between you and your supplier in an instant. Meanwhile, you've freed up all those resources to invest in your core activities.

Ask yourself

Are we performing tasks in-house which we could more profitably outsource to a supplier with an Internet link? What could we do with the resources we would liberate?

Idea 31 – Lonely business hearts

You don't have to go it alone. It's a big, World Wide Web out there for one company to cope with by itself. So how about finding a partner? Partnership deals have never been so easy to find, and the Internet is the perfect place to look for them.

Maybe you're a manufacturer and you'd like to go into partnership with a retail business rather than set up your own retail arm. Or perhaps you want to pair up with a business with the computer know-how to boost your profits. Perhaps you'd like the attentions of an investor in order to expand (for venture capital, see *Idea*

43). Or maybe you want to get it together with another similar business overseas and distribute each other's goods.

Whatever kind of partnership deal you're looking for, the Internet is the place to find it. Organisations like Fourleaf.com, among others, operate as a dating agency for their members, putting them in touch with other businesses who are looking for corporate investment, joint venturing, acquisitions and strategic alliances. So don't get lonely in cyberspace; find yourself an exciting new partner.

Eleven Greatest Ideas for Promoting your Internet Business

It doesn't matter how great your Web site is, and how desirable the products and services it sells; no one's going to visit it if they don't know it's there. So arguably the best way to make money from an Internet business is to promote it. You can do this by straight advertising, of course (*Idea 32*), and also by making mutually beneficial advertising arrangements with other Web sites (*Ideas 33* and *34*).

But advertising is by no means the only way to let people know you're out there. *Ideas 35–39* will get you free publicity online, as would *Idea 40* for those unscrupulous enough to use it.

But perhaps one of the most essential methods of attracting people to your site is through search engines. If anyone is looking for your type of product or service and enters relevant keywords into the search engine, it will give them a list of all the sites on its listing which match with those keywords. Trouble is, there might be thousands, and yours might be number 237,000 on the list. That's going to take a while to scroll down to. So *Idea 41* deals with the essential matter of how to get your Web site listed high on the search engines.

And finally, why is it that so many businesses with an Internet arm forget about it in the rest of their dealings? Even businesses which operate exclusively online often seem to forget about their activities which happen in the real world rather than the virtual one – things like invoices and deliveries, recruitment ads and office stationery. Take a look at *Idea 42* to make sure you don't miss any opportunities to promote your business offline.

Whatever method of promotion you use, however, remember one thing. Your Web site must deliver what the advertising and promotion promises, or you won't get any benefit from the new visitors you attract. They will go away without buying, and they won't come back. They won't come back even if you improve your Web site, because they won't know you've improved it – or they won't care. So don't start trying to pull in customers until you're quite certain that you can impress them once they arrive, with both your Web site and the products and services you sell on it.

Idea 32 – Fly the flag (or the banner)

Half the money I spend on advertising is wasted. The trouble is I never know which half.

Lord
Leverhulme

The most obvious form of advertising on the Web, and the most frequently used, is banner ads. Your banner appears on someone else's Web site, and anyone can simply click on the ad to link through to your Web site. Banner ads are generally paid for by impression. That means that every time someone calls up the page with your banner ad on it, you pay. You can advertise on search engines, specialist sites, local directories, top 100 sites or anywhere else that will have you.

However, what many people don't seem to realise is that banner advertising isn't all that it's cracked up to be. The most critical question is: how many people who see your banner will click on it? And the answer is that click-through rates have been dropping for a while now. There was a time when the average click-through rate was one in fifty; now it's nearer one in two hundred. Considering the cost of banner advertising, this can make it a very expensive way to do business.

On the other hand, banner advertising does put your name in front of potential visitors in a way which can be very hard to achieve otherwise. So do you give up on it completely, or is there an alternative? Here are a few tips for making banner advertising pay:

- Use targeted advertising. You'll get a much better response rate if you advertise on specialist sites which are related to your own, or on local directories if you are advertising a local business or service. If you advertise on search engines, go for what are known as ROC ads – run-of-category ads. These are not run throughout the entire site, but only on specific sections or categories; a keyword purchase will buy you advertising only when users key in a specified keyword that is relevant to your site. This is more expensive than run-of-site ads, but also far more closely targeted.

- Consider spending your money at four or five smaller (and therefore cheaper) Web sites, rather than splashing out for a presence on one heavy-traffic site. If you go for niche content sites, a user with an interest in the subject will see your ads on every relevant site they visit.

- Try to pay per click, per lead or per customer, rather than per impression. In other words, you only have to pay when a user actually clicks through to your site, or places an order. If you're a fairly small set-up you may have difficulty persuading the top Internet sites to change their system to suit you, I grant you. But if they won't, think hard before you advertise with them. The word is that this type of payment is going to become much more popular on the Net, and soon, as the smart companies are getting wise to the limitations of traditional pay-per-impression banner advertising.

If you follow these guidelines to make banner advertising cost effective, make sure you design an ad that will pull people in:

- It needs to be animated or interactive for a start; static ads just don't get the response rates.
- Invite the customer to do something, from asking a question which they need to click to find the answer to, to incorporating a drop-down menu.
- Keep the design simple.
- Make it clear what you are advertising.
- Include the words 'click here'.

It *is* possible to bring in worthwhile business using banner ads; just follow these guidelines to avoid making the same mistakes most other people do.

Ask yourself

Could we spend our advertising money more effectively than through banner advertising? If not, how can we target our prospects most tightly on the Net?

Idea 33 – Two's company

Lots of online businesses out there are attracting just the customers *you* want. What's more, most of them aren't even competitors. It's not fair! Why should extremesports.co.uk have countless visitors checking out their dangerous sports videos, books, clothing and courses, when none of them knows about your fabulous site selling surfboards and wetsuits?

One solution to this problem is to set up an affiliate program (also known as an associate program). The way it works is that extremesports.co.uk provides a link from their site to yours, in exchange for a commission of some kind. You might pay them for the traffic that clicks through, or a commission on sales generated as a result. It makes their site more appealing – they can now offer their visitors somewhere to buy surfboards online – and you have a foot in the door to attract all those Websurfing surfers you knew were out there.

And why stop at extremesports.co.uk? You can set up a whole network of affiliate programs to bring in new visitors. Many specialists now argue that this is the most effective way to make your online business grow fast.

The first ever affiliate program was launched by Amazon.com in 1997. Mind you, although it is very successful, it has its problems. For example, Amazon pay their affiliates – who are generally specialist booksellers – a commission for sales following a click-through. But many customers don't buy straight away. They come back later, going direct to Amazon, and there's no commission for the affiliate. So to keep your affiliates happy, you need to think through your proposed system thoroughly (and see *Idea 67*).

Here are a few pointers to potential trouble spots to avoid:

- Make sure you have the technical and legal aspects well tied up. There's plenty of software available; just make sure you buy the software that really does the job you need, not just the cheapest you can get.
- Use a commission system which benefits both you and your affiliates. They won't stay with you long if the program doesn't benefit both of you.
- You need to check out potential affiliates so that you can avoid the ones whose Web sites you wouldn't want to be associated with, or who aren't going to give you the quality or quantity of traffic you want.
- You will have to establish an accounting system which tracks visitors and sales, and which your affiliates can check online to see what their commission status is.
- Build a good relationship with your affiliates. Send them regular reports and cheques, provide technical support for them, and train them to help them maximise your sales.

Here's the twist

Bear in mind that you won't attract affiliates unless they like both you and your product, and think that you have the potential to make plenty of sales. They need to assess you as much as you do them. A good affiliate, with a high-traffic site, is going to be in demand. They can't promote everyone, so they will constantly be comparing you with other potential affiliates to see if you are worth staying with.

Idea 34 – Criss-cross

Affiliate programs are one idea for attracting visitors via other sites – here's another. Look for sites which will attract the same type of visitors as you and which would benefit from a link from your site. Then offer to set up a cross-link, where you each add a link to the other one's site.

This idea is obviously at its most promising when both sites attract a roughly comparable number of visitors. If the other site gets half a million hits a day and you get fifty, they might feel that there wasn't much in it for them.

Idea 35 – Ring ring

Web rings are lists of Web sites which are grouped together by interest. You enrol, and then get added into the ring. It's free to join, and it attracts high quality traffic as people travel the rings on the subjects that they are interested in. Check it out on www.webring.org.

Idea 36 – Be a journalist

There are plenty of ezines out there looking for articles to run. Just as you would write a press release and circulate it to offline newspapers and magazines, you can do the same thing online. Find out where the most promising ezines are (try BestEzines.com, E-Zine-List and eZine search), and circulate press releases and feature articles that promote you and your Web site.

Idea 37 – Post a newsgroup

There are over 20,000 newsgroups on the Net, and millions of participants every day. They are bulletin boards where people can communicate with each other, accessed via a news server. Blatant advertising is not welcomed on most newsgroups, but you can join in discussions and sign yourself with a tag line which briefly describes your Internet business and Web address.

Obviously you'll want to contact newsgroups which cover topics related to your business. Monitor the newsgroup for a while, and make sure there are plenty of genuine users – some newsgroups have become little more than commercial advertising sites. If you become a regular participant, always mentioning your Web site as you sign off, you will become known by the other newsgroup members and you will build your credibility and attract visitors to the site.

To locate relevant newsgroups, try www.deja.com or www.forumone.com.

> *Ask yourself*
>
> What newsgroups might be interested in our product or service?

Idea 38 – Email lists

An email list is similar to a newsgroup, except that messages go directly to the participants' email boxes rather than to a newsgroup which they have to visit in order to read them. The same rules apply to promoting your business through email lists as through newsgroups.

You might want to check out directories of email lists: www.liszt.com and www.neoserv.com's list of Publicly Accessible Mailing Lists.

Idea 39 – Roll up! Roll up!

Why not host events on your Web site? You can attract visitors by running competitions and games, online interviews, audio broadcasts or chat sessions (see *Idea 69*). You'll need to promote these on and offline, but they are a great way of bringing people in, especially a little while after a Web site launch when traffic starts to tail off.

Idea 40 – The cheat's approach to hoodwinking newsgroups

Having looked at outlets for promoting your business online, here's one way not to do it. Newsgroups and forums have fairly strict codes of conduct, and they don't like being taken for a ride. This means that if you do it and get caught, you're going to severely jeopardise your credibility and your chances of ever marketing to a newsgroup again.

However, I've decided that this technique deserves a mention in this book since it is certainly an idea for making money on the Internet, albeit a very underhand one. And it certainly works … *if* you don't get caught. So here's the crack.

The trick is to assume several identities, using your friends' accounts. So you post to your chosen newsgroup – or to several – using the first identity. For example, to a gardening newsgroup:

Can anyone help me find a really nifty little gadget I read about recently? It's a trowel which has some kind of fold-out gardener's knife concealed in the handle. I saw it somewhere a few weeks ago – it might have been posted in the group – but now I've decided I want one, I can't track it down.

Next, you use another friend's account to post a further comment:

> *I know what you're talking about. I've seen it advertised but I can't remember where. I noticed it because it looked really useful. I think the tip of the trowel had prongs, which doubled as a hand fork. Let me know if you ever track it down.*

The next posting from another account goes something like this:

> *I've just bought one of them. It's called a Garden Helper and it's great. It's got a special gadget, which automatically sharpens the knife every time you fold it away. I think it cost about £15, and I got it from www._____ but you might be able to get it at a big garden centre.*

Idea 41 – Be search engine friendly

Search engines are the gateways – or portals to use Internet-speak – to the Web. Many Web surfers start with search engines, such as AltaVista or Excite, to find a Web site that provides what they are looking for. They do this by entering key words that relate to their search, and the search engine replies with a list of sites which may number anything from none or one to hundreds of thousands.

You definitely want to be listed on the search engines. Apart from anything else, it costs nothing to be listed. Search engines work by using indexing software agents called robots or spiders. These constantly spider the Web looking for new or updated pages to add to their listings. They will check the lead or home page, and generally go down one level further, indexing the pages for keyword searches. But if your Web site is several levels deep it's worth realising that spiders are unlikely to index right through it. Although these spiders should find you eventually, it's worth short-cutting the exercise by submitting your lead page to the search engines to be sure that they are listed.

The most important thing is to appear within the first few pages of the listings for the keywords you appear under, rather than on page four thousand. The search engine will rank matches in order of importance/relevance, but they don't disclose their exact criteria, and they change them quite frequently. So how can you make sure that your site gets a high ranking?

You need to start by submitting your site to the search engines. You can use a free automated submission service such as *Postmaster* or *Submit It* to list your site with up to about 400 search engines. But each search engine has different variables, such as the maximum number of characters in the title. So the most effective approach is manually to submit the information to each search engine individually – at least the major search engines. The statistic often quoted is that you will get about five times the traffic via search engines if you submit manually, or using sophisticated submission software, rather than using a submission service. Of course, it will take you a lot longer.

The way you submit your site to a search engine is page by page (not that you have to submit every page). You should at least submit your home page, but the search engine will only list what you have submitted, so if certain keywords don't appear on your home page, you won't get listed even if another page of your site is relevant. So submit as many pages as you need to get you maximum coverage – at least your home page and your main section pages.

When you submit your web pages, you have to submit (among other things, such as your business name and so on) the full page URL, the page title, a brief description of the page, and relevant keywords. So how can you optimise your search engine ranking?

Title

The aim is to include, throughout your submission, the keywords which people are likely to use to search. Make sure the page title includes keywords and descriptive information. When your page is listed on the search engine, the title will be displayed, so make sure it is as descriptive and as helpful as possible to attract the user to it.

Keywords

Different search engines allow you to list a different number of keywords. List the keywords that you think people will enter in the search engine. Unless a topic is very specific, a single word search gives far too many results, so most people key in two or three word phrases rather than single words. Think what these might be and include them in your keywords. Here are a few more tips:

- If a searcher is likely to use upper case letters or plurals, include these in your keywords.
- If searchers are likely to misspell a word – such as 'stationary' instead of 'stationery' – include the misspelt version in some of your pages.
- Test your keywords by doing a keyword search and seeing how many results come up. If there are too many, include phrases that searchers might use to narrow down the results.
- Search engines will look to see how often the keywords appear on your page, and assign importance to the page in this way. So you want to repeat your keywords. However, they are wise to people including keywords too often simply as a ruse to get placed higher, so some search engines will downgrade you for overuse of keywords – more than about half a dozen uses per page.
- Search engines are more interested in text near the top of the page; some virtually ignore wording beyond the first couple of paragraphs. So make sure that the important text and keywords are near the top of the page, and keep your pages relatively short. Most search engines display the first few lines of text, so try to make sure they say something that will encourage the user to click on your site.

Metatags

A metatag is a series of HTML lines at the top of almost every web page. It contains the information about that page, including its title, description and keywords; this is where those little spiders gather their information from. Some search engines look for metatag 'title', 'description' and 'keywords', which agree with each other and with the body text on the page.

If you change your 'title' metatag, visiting spiders will think they are visiting a new page, and index it again. This can give you multiple listings of the same page under different titles, which is a good thing.

You can also check out your competitors' metatags to see what title and keywords they are using. Download the page in question – maybe the one at the top of the search engine list you are further down on – and click on 'view' on your browser's toolbar. Then click on 'source'. This will show you their source codes, with their metatags at the top of the page.

Don't use frames

Spiders won't follow links that are in frames. If your opening page uses frames, they will not find anything else on your site.

Don't spam the search engines

Some search engines will not allow you to submit more than one page a day; they regard this as spamming. Others will allow you to make multiple submissions. So make sure you stay on the right side of each search engine. Spamming also covers the very silly practice of including keywords which have nothing to do with your site

– such as 'sex' – simply to attract visitors. If you haven't got what they're looking for, they won't buy. You want targeted visitors who are genuine hot prospects.

Request links with other sites

Some search engines give priority to sites that have links to other sites. So make sure that you will still get a high ranking if this criterion is being used.

Once you have submitted your site, don't just leave it there. Keep checking your ranking (you can get software to do this for you) and, most especially, check that you are higher up the listings than your competitors. Your prospects are going to check out the first site they find, so it had better be yours. If you find you're slipping down the search engine, see if you can change your pages in some way to improve your ranking again. In any case update your submissions regularly as you add material to your Web site. You can also buy software which helps you to optimise your search engine ranking.

Ask yourself

Do we know how many of our visitors come to us via search engines? How can we improve this figure?

Idea 42 – Get real!

Don't forget that there's a whole, real world out there. Just because you're attracting people to do business online, it doesn't mean you have to find them online.

There are all sorts of ways to promote your Web site offline, whether you operate exclusively on the Web or whether your Web site is just one arm of your business.

For a start offline PR, from launch events to press releases, will help to bring people to your site. And you can make sure that your staff tell customers about it regularly. And why not direct enquiries for general information to your Web site too? If someone calls up for a brochure, offer them a choice: would they like the brochure in the post tomorrow, or would they prefer to have a look at your Web site now?

And don't miss an opportunity to publicise your Web site address. Even if people don't remember the address exactly, at least they'll know you have one. Here are a few places you can splash it:

- letterheads and comp slips;
- invoices;
- delivery notes;
- brochures and catalogues;
- instruction leaflets;
- corporate Christmas cards;
- your answerphone message;
- company vehicles (how about large print right down the side of your vans?);
- advertisements; and
- recruitment ads.

If you want your customers to deal with you online, make sure they know you're there and can find you. Keep your name in front of them, on and offline, and you'll find the business will start rolling in.

Ask yourself

Are we displaying our Web site address everywhere we can?

Five Greatest Ideas for Starting Up and Selling an Internet Business

If you're not yet an Internet millionaire (and I guess if you're reading this you're not), don't give up hope. Right now, it's far from impossible. And what's more, many of the most successful entrepreneurs started out with little experience and no money. Sure it helps to pull in investment (and following *Ideas 43* and *44* will help), but it can be done without. Or if you do have some money to put into a business, why not buy a franchise (*Idea 45*)?

And once you've got your business up and running successfully, that's the time to sell it for millions to some incredibly rich business that is really taken by your energy and vision. *Ideas 46* and *47* will give you some tips for doing just that.

In the meantime, while you're waiting to make your first million, it may come as some comfort to reflect on the fact that most of the Internet millionaires you read about aren't nearly as rich as you think (OK, I'm not including Bill Gates here). The reason is that in order to be sure of their investment, investors expect you to leave your shares in the business and to continue to work for it. After all, a lot of what they're paying for is likely to be your vision, so they need you there to see it through.

They expect you to work extremely hard and to draw a salary that is comfortable but no more for several years. Then if – and it can be a big if – the business does really well, it can be floated on the stock exchange. But to attract shareholders, the owners have to show they are committed by hanging on to their shares for several more years. Eventually, if the company continues to thrive, they can cash in some or all of their shares. But real money-in-the-bank wealth is several years down the line. So by the time the next new Internet millionaire you read about is actually in a position to flash a wad of readies, you'll have had time to make your first million too.

Idea 43 – Be on the side of the angels

Venture capital – two of the most exciting words if you're planning to make millions out of an Internet business idea. Venture capitalists invest literally billions every year in new businesses; they are the business angels who can make you rich.

Venture capital is a form of investment in which the venture firm gives you capital – usually for a specified period such as three to five years – in exchange for a share in the business, which includes a degree of control. At the end of the specified period the venture capitalist can exit (to use the jargon) through a buyout, a merger or acquisition, or public flotation. A venture capitalist is looking for a business that will give them a return when they exit of five to ten times their original investment. Venture capitalists might be pension funds, insurance companies, corporations, foundations or individuals.

Money is better than poverty, if only for finan- cial reasons.

Woody Allen

But there's always a downside, of course. The bad news is that they receive literally thousands of applications for funding every year. They interview maybe one in fifty of the applicants, and fund perhaps a few dozen businesses each year. However, somebody has to be a winner, so why shouldn't it be you? The question you need answered is: what are venture capitalists looking for?

Clearly, they must be looking for a combination of factors to be able to sift maybe 5000 applicants down to perhaps 30 businesses to invest in. And *you* are one of the most critical factors of all. Venture capitalists are looking for businesses that are run by people who are completely committed to the business. They want to see that you have found the time to start your business despite having a full-time job – or that you have already given up your job to dedicate yourself to the business. They want to see that you will work all the hours it takes to get the business working. They need to see that you have a vision for the business, and an emotional stake in making it work. In other words, they need to be certain that if they give you the money you want, your commitment won't wane.

A lot of investors take the view that ideas are ten a penny, but people who are able to convert a good idea into a successful business are like gold dust. So they give high priority to your ability to demonstrate the right skills and commitment.

What do they want?

It's hard to over-emphasise the importance of you and the other key people whose skills you can call on. You should have a strong management team, but one which is still flexible enough for an investor to influence. But apart from the impression which you personally need to make on potential investors, what about your business idea? What are they looking for there?

If you're trying to make money on the Internet, or in an Internet-related business, you're off to a good start. The vast majority of venture capital funding these days goes into technology companies. But apart from this, the key factors most venture capitalists will look for are:

- a business which can be built up relatively inexpensively;
- a clear distribution channel;
- a potential to become a market leader;
- an ability to generate gross margins of over 50 per cent; and
- an ability to grow to a value of at least £10–15 million in the next five years, with an eventual value of at least £30 million.

When you make a presentation to a venture capitalist, they will want to see a well put-together business plan (see *Idea 44*). They will ask you all sorts of questions about:

- your product or service;
- yourselves;

- your business;
- your current financial arrangements;
- your customers;
- your industry;
- your competitors;
- your marketing plan; and
- your growth potential.

You need to be fully conversant in every aspect of your business idea in order to impress these people. Be prepared to back up your answers with hard facts and evidence; statistics about industry trends, prepared charts and graphs, cost details, competitors annual reports ... in other words demonstrate that you have done all your research and you really know what you're talking about.

What do they expect in return?

The general rule of thumb is that the earlier in the life of your business the venture capitalists invest, the greater percentage of the company they want in return, because their risk is higher. So the longer you can keep going without them, and the greater customer base and turnover you can build up, the less of your business you will have to give away when the time comes. If a venture capitalist puts in, say, half the value of the business, they might expect to take about a third of it. So if it is worth £1 million on paper, and they put in £0.5 million, you would typically be left with about two thirds of your company.

Venture capitalists also like to have a say in who runs the company they are investing in. So while you want to show that you have people on board with experience in all the necessary areas, it is a mistake to present potential investors with a complete management team. They will want you to give some kind of stock options to top managers, to ensure their commitment to building the company – up to about ten per cent to a managing director, and as much as three per cent for other top managers.

Does all this make you feel you're losing control? Well, you may well do. And that's one of the minus points for many people. By the time your company finally goes public, you will probably own no more than 20 per cent of it. Some entrepreneurs end up with as little as three per cent. But hey, even that could make you a fortune if all goes well.

Just show me the money

So where can you find likely venture capitalists to invest in your business? There are various sites that will help you; try www.vfinance.com or www.financehub.com for listings of venture capital firms, along with other resources such as articles and guides to attracting venture capital.

Another option is to sign up with what is known as a business incubator. These organisations help you set up and nurture an online business. They give you help building your site, setting up an online shop and getting a merchant account. They will also offer you consultancy and, if you want, guide you to attract venture capital. Try www.business-incubator.com or www.enformatica.com.

Idea 44 – The plan of action

The key document that will attract investors or buyers of any kind to your business is your business plan. The mere words 'business plan' tend to make most people's hearts sink. A business plan seems to imply endless work in order to produce a dry, turgid document at the end, which you mostly made up anyway so you don't even believe in it.

I'm not going to pretend that writing a business plan is as exciting as winning a fortnight's holiday for two in the Maldives. But the fortnight you invest in writing it could eventually – who knows – bring you in enough money to retire to the Maldives. And actually, once you get into it, it can be fascinating. Writing a business plan for your own business is much more rewarding than writing anyone else's. It's all about your business idea, how you can make it work, and how much it's worth. Just the sort of thing you're probably happy to talk about for hours. Now you just have to write it down.

Good business leaders create a vision, articulate the vision, passionately own the vision, and relentlessly drive it to completion.

Jack Welch

If you can afford it, and you really feel your writing and presentation skills are atrocious, you can pay a professional to write the plan for you. But you should be involved in the research, because if you are asked questions about the plan by investors – and you will be – you must be totally clued up on it. A good compromise is to prepare all the material yourself and then pay a professional to put it down on the page for you.

So what's the plan?

Many people fret about writing business plans simply because they don't really have a clue what a business plan is supposed to look like and what goes in it. If this is you, don't worry. You're in the majority. But it's really pretty straightforward. There are seven sections that you need to cover:

1   Introduction
2   The business
3   The market
4   Development
5   The marketing plan
6   Management structure
7   Financial information.

1 Introduction

This bit's a breeze. At the very beginning of the business plan you need to include all the basic information which your reader – the investor or buyer – will want to know. There are generally three pages in this section:

- *The cover sheet* should look professional and attractive, and include the words 'business plan' prominently, along with your business name. It should also include, perhaps at the bottom or in a corner, your own name, company logo, business address, phone, fax and email numbers.
- *The contents sheet* is just that, to help readers find their way around the document quickly.
- *The executive summary* is a short summary of the whole document, which should fit comfortably on a single page. It is the first thing potential investors or buyers will read, and if they're not impressed by it, it will be the last thing they read too. It needs to contain the key facts – what the business is, why it has potential, what investment you are looking for, how this will help the business grow. It should make the reader want to read the rest of the plan, but it shouldn't be written in a hard-sell style. Oh and, by the way, it comes at the beginning but you will find it much easier to write it last of all.

2 The business

This section is a description of the business, as you would imagine. Start with a single sentence, which encapsulates what the business is there for, and who it is targeted at. Then you need to state what the business does, what its products or services are, why this has market appeal and why the business will succeed. Make your products or services sound interesting, and explain what makes them so good. You will also need to include a description of what your pricing structure will be, how you arrived at it and why it is the right one.

You will need to include an industry overview here – industry trends and so on. Back these up with hard, quotable facts such as 'According to XYZ Industry Research Co., this industry is expanding by 80 per cent a year, and the trend is predicted to continue for at least a further ten years.'

3 *The market*

The aim here is to demonstrate that there are plenty of people out there ready to buy from you. So describe the type of customer for whom your products or services are intended. Then state (and justify with facts and figures) how many such people there are – what the size of the market is. Discuss the key competitors with whom you have to share this market, and estimate (with reasons) your own likely share of the market. Include your projected sales for the next three years, broken down by quarters.

When it comes to discussing competitors, by the way, don't slate them. Stick to facts. Say what their turnover is, what their market share is, and how satisfied their customers are with them. Explain where they have weaknesses that you can exploit.

4 *Development*

This is the section where you can explain the actual running of the business. Start with your current position, whether this is just an idea or whether you are already running the business, and what size and stage it is at. Specify what else you need, and when you will be ready to begin trading if you aren't already.

Now explain the process of the business – how you produce the goods or deliver the service. What actually goes on between when a customer places an order and when you deliver?

This section should also include details and costs of product development, production facilities, physical location, staffing, capital investments and operating expenses.

5 *The marketing plan*

How are you going to persuade people to buy from you? Explain how you will target prospects – online or offline, through affiliates or whatever. Discuss any market opportunities and how you will exploit them, and also include the main threats, or minus points (such as high costs, poor response, strong competition), and discuss how you will counter them.

Specify what your advertising and promotion plans are. For example, where are you going to advertise (not every ad, but whether you will focus on search engines, the industry press, TV ads or whatever)? And what about press releases? Special events? Trade shows? Again, don't give lists of details, but state, for example, that you will attend five trade shows a year, including the three top shows in the industry.

6 *Management structure*

Who is running your business? Start with the main positions in the company. Explain who is filling them, and what their credentials are (include a CV for each, in an appendix). If any positions are vacant, give a job description.

Explain who owns the business at the moment, and who is on the board of directors. Include all their connections, experience and track record to persuade investors that they are real assets.

You can also build your credibility if you can list good support services such as accountants, lawyers, advisers and so on.

7 *Financial information*

This section should include the business basics: cash flow forecast, balance sheet, profit and loss account. You should also identify the financial risks you face – every business has them, and investors need to know that you recognise them.

Finally, if you're after investment rather than purchase, specify what kind of funding you need, how much, and precisely what you are going to do with it. This is important to getting investors to stump up the cash. They also like to see that you are prepared to put your own money on the line. And show them how they can get out of the arrangement in, say, five years time. Persuade them that the business will be saleable or floatable so that they can cash in their investment.

How does it look?

A business plan must be a professional document if it is going to attract professional funding. So make sure it looks smart. That means smart page layout, plenty of sub-headings so the reader can navigate the document easily, and perfect spelling, punctuation and grammar. This is where you should get as many friends and colleagues as possible to read it for you, make corrections and tell you if anything is unclear.

Your business plan can make or break your bid for funding. If it isn't up to scratch, you will probably never even get a personal meeting with an investor. If it is thoroughly professional and persuasive, it could set you on your way to your first million.

Idea 45 – Buy into success

If you've got the money to start a business – maybe redundancy money – but you haven't got a really marketable idea, why not buy someone else's? There are plenty of Web sites and Internet businesses up for sale (see *Idea 46*). You simply need to find a business that you believe you can make a success of.

If you're thinking of buying an Internet business, you'll need to consider several questions, such as:

- Why is the business up for sale?
- What has its history been?
- What has its business and marketing strategy been?
- How does the current owner believe the business could expand?

Following on from *Idea 44*, you will of course want to see a professional business plan from the seller. But above all, if you're looking for a business to buy and run yourself, rather than one to invest in, make sure it is selling something that you can get enthusiastic about. To succeed, you're going to have to devote a very high proportion of your waking life to this – you really don't want to be bored by it. Best of all is to try and find a business that involves a favourite hobby or pursuit ... just don't let your enthusiasm blind you to any flaws in the business plan.

The good news is that there are plenty of Web sites that have been set up by people who have a good basic idea, but then lack either the resources or the skills to make a real success out of it. These businesses are not necessarily very expensive to buy, and if you can invest the time and management skills that the present owner lacks – well, you could build a thriving business on the back of someone else's idea.

Idea 46 – Let them know you're selling

If you have a thriving Web site you may be lucky enough to be approached by an interested buyer. But in the real world, you generally have to go out there and look for someone to buy your Web site. If you think your Web site is worth billions, you will probably want to bring in expensive professionals to help you sell it. But if you don't think this expense is justified, one of the best ideas is to go to a Web site broker.

Web site brokers buy and sell Web sites on the Net. They all offer similar but not identical services, generally including:

- services for both buyers and sellers;

- listings of Web sites for sale;
- valuation service;
- resources such as links to related articles; and
- facilities to look up and register domain names (and see *Idea 60*).

It is often free to list your Web site for sale, and you pay a commission to the broker if it sells through them. One such broker is at www.WebSiteBroker.com; they also include a listing of other Web site brokers.

Idea 47 – Have grown-ups on the team

If you *are* a grown-up, you can skip on to the next section. But if you're young and fresh with a great Internet business to sell, you may need to find a grown-up first. Whether you want funding or whether you want to sell up and retire, you need to impress investors. And while investors may *say* that they love your young, fresh approach, deep down it makes them nervous.

They just aren't certain that you have the management skills and experience to back up the business. They want the best of both worlds. They want you young, fresh ... and experienced. The answer to this problem is to bring someone else on board who has the necessary qualifications. It might be an investment banker you've persuaded to join the team, or a senior manager with a track record of successes. Financial people certainly impress investors – money is what they're all about after all.

Of course, you can bring in more than one grown-up. But you should give them a share in the business so that they are clearly an integral part of it, not just an employee or an adviser. Your potential investors are likely to be older and more experienced than you, so give them someone they can chat to over dinner who remembers what it was like in the old days before the World Wide Web was invented.

Six Greatest Ideas for Choosing an Internet Business

When you start a business, you obviously want to sell something that lots of people will want to buy. Of course there are plenty of highly successful businesses selling into niche markets, but if you want to maximise your chances of making a fortune, you could do worse than go where you know the money is.

The good news for anyone who isn't full of inspirational new ideas is that the most successful sites are not generally the most original. The majority of top Internet businesses operate in the same markets, although of course some of them have an original twist to them, as you'll see in *Ideas 51–53*. The most popular sites of all are the pornography sites (surprise, surprise), but if you're going for a more respectable business, by far the best-selling products on the Net are software and information.

There is a strong challenge here, however. On the Web, there is a mighty advantage to be had from being first in the field. In both information and software, this is getting increasingly hard. There are still new types of information to peddle, and new angles on selling software, but it's getting tougher to find them. And, of course, there is money to be made in other fields too. What is certain is that if you really want to make a fortune, you need to think – and research – hard about the kind of Internet business you launch.

Idea 48 – Stick to one idea

Suppose you run a business that manufactures garden fencing. You've been running the business for a while, and you've added a few other lines. Maybe you built a few garden buildings – summer houses and gazebos – using your fencing panels, so you diversified into designing garden buildings. And perhaps you also have a profitable sideline hiring out chain link fencing sections to construction firms to protect their building sites. So now you have three separate operations running under one roof. And you want to set up a Web site to sell online.

Don't assume you can successfully transfer your three-pronged business as it is. The thing is, it is much harder to attract people's attention with an online business. It won't be difficult with your existing customers whom you direct to your Web site, but attracting new customers online requires a very specific, simple message.

A lot of customers will arrive via search engines and banner ads, where you have only a few words to attract their attention and explain who you are and what you do. You will simply muddy the picture if you try to explain that you sell garden fencing, hire out construction site fencing *and* design gazebos ... all in the space of a couple of lines.

So formulate one clear message and stick to it. Look at the banner ads that you see online and notice how the best ones take a maximum of a few words to explain the business. Either create a single umbrella message, which describes all your functions – fences and buildings – or create separate Web sites. It doesn't matter if you are technically running a single business, you can still have several Web sites (presumably advertising each other if the products are at all related). So you might have one fencing Web site and one garden buildings design site; each will have a different name that reflects its content.

It is a mistake to try to spread your message too thinly; pick one very clear, concise image and stick to it. That way you are more likely to build two or three successful Web sites, instead of one underperforming site.

Ask yourself

Do all our products and services fit comfortably together under an umbrella banner, or might we do better if we promoted totally separate functions through separate Web sites?

Idea 49 – Never mind the end customer, what about the advertisers?

You must have noticed how many free services there are on the Internet. You can find out all sorts of information, from business advice to where to eat out, and no one seems to expect you to pay for it. You can download the complete works of Shakespeare, or be emailed a recipe for every day of the year, and it won't cost you a penny. How do they do it?

The answer of course is advertising. Most sites that offer free information work in a similar way to free local newspapers. The fact that you and others visit them makes them an appealing prospect to advertisers.

Information-based sites are among the most prolific on the Web, and are often the most lucrative too. So if you want to start a Web site, you don't necessarily need a product or service to sell. If you can set up a free information site, you could still rake it in. Here are the most important guidelines for making the site profitable:

1 Choose a topic that is in demand, and preferably one that isn't out there already so you can be the first – always a huge advantage on the Net. You might hold the ultimate reference site on plants and trees of the world, or you might list every source of car spares in any locality. And think about who the big advertisers are whom you might attract; pick a field where there's plenty of advertising money around. Have a surf to see what's out there so that you get an idea of the sort of sites that are popular.

2 Bear in mind what the advertisers want. They want you to have as many visitors as possible, obviously, and they also want the right type of visitors – the ones with money to spend. They want quality as well as quantity. Sites that appeal to young people are popular, as are sites that are targeted at 30–40 year olds. Even better if the subject of your site is likely to appeal particularly to people with a disposable income – a site for classic car collectors perhaps, or yachting enthusiasts, or people who play the stock markets.

3   You'll need to promote your site well initially – either on or offline – in order to build up the kind of visitor levels that will attract advertisers.

4   The more pages your site has, the more ads it can carry.

5   Your income may come from advertisers, but their enthusiasm for advertising is going to be entirely dependent on the quality and quantity of people who visit your site. So you need to focus on providing the best possible service for your users, even though they pay you nothing, in order to encourage them to keep revisiting your site. Always be looking for new channels of information to offer, and ways to make the site easier and more fun to use.

Information sites that generate their income through advertising take time and money to set up. You are unlikely to see a significant income in the first six months. But these sites can turn into big earners, and once running they are relatively low-maintenance. You don't have any of the production, order taking and delivery headaches that most organisations do. If you have enough visitors, you don't even have to sell the ads yourself, you can find brokers to do it for you.

Many people run these kinds of sites in a few hours a week on top of full-time jobs. As a rough guide, if you attract around 10,000 visitors a month you might expect to sell banner ads at, say, £150 a page. If you have twenty pages, that's an income of around £3000 a month. And if the site grows ... well, the top sites are charging tens of thousands of pounds for a single ad. Before long, it could be you.

Ask yourself

How much is our customer base worth to advertisers?

Idea 50 – There's money in adult sites

When the Internet first started to take off, pornographers clearly thought it had been designed for them. And it's easy to see why – from the privacy of their own homes their customers can download pornographic images of just about any kind – from the mildly erotic to the positively illegal, and it is almost impossible for anyone to trace them. Consequently, adult sites have been around longer than almost any others, and are at the cutting edge of new Internet technology, from keyboard chats to live broadcasts online. Adult sites are the most fully developed sector of e-commerce, with high numbers of actual buyers and plenty of sellers – dozens of new sites open every week.

Like it or not, there's no denying that selling pornography online was one of the best ever ideas for making money on the Internet. But if, like me, you find some aspects of the industry extremely distasteful, you may still be attracted to setting up a site that operates on a more acceptable periphery of the industry.

To give you an example, many psychologists now believe that sex can become an addiction. Some Web sites now exist to help people cope with the addiction, or to point them to various sources of help. Another important development in the sex industry is that women are now making up a much larger proportion of the buying public; sites aimed specifically at women are likely to prosper. And romance rather than hard porn is certainly popular in the book market – in the US, sales of romantic novels now make up almost half of all paperback sales. Perhaps this market could be expanded on the Web.

One of the reasons for the growth in the sex industry – on and offline – is reckoned to be the increase in AIDS and other sexually transmitted diseases. Virtual sex is just about the most reliable form of safe sex. Internet businesses could address this more directly, perhaps incorporating advice

In truth, I believe there is no such thing as a growth industry. There are only companies organised and operated to create and capitalise on growth opportunities. Industries that assume themselves to be riding some automatic growth escalator invariably descend into stagnation.

Theodore Levitt

and facts on safe sex with the sale of condoms and other products that make sex safer.

Adult sites are the most successful sites out there in terms of generating cash, so even if you don't want to get your hands dirty, so to speak, you can still learn from them.

Idea 51 – Information sites #1: Student-Net

One of the best ways to give you a clue as to the kind of site that could make you a fortune is to give you real examples of sites that have already made their originators a fortune. So here are three of my favourite new information-based Internet businesses.

First up is a site called Student-Net, which is a real fantasy success story. It all sprang from an idea that student Peter Atalia had while he was cleaning his teeth. Peter was a student at Nottingham Trent University, and trying to find somewhere to live. He thought how useful it would be if he could find a flat on the Internet. There was no site that could help, which is what made him think that perhaps he and a few mates could start one.

He talked to three of his fellow students and, after they left university, they launched Student-Net.co.uk. To begin with, they simply listed accommodation in Nottingham, but then expanded into information about courses, health, finance, and shops and pubs in the city. They even added a free dating service. Within a few months, they were clocking up about 20,000 visits a week, many from people who didn't even live in Nottingham. And within months, it had attracted the interest of the International Media Products Group in Nevada, who bought a controlling share of the business for £10 million, in order to expand it to cover university life worldwide.

The four founders went from living in digs on student loans to running an international business in the space of six months – by which time their average age was just 22.

Ask yourself

What information do you need yourself, which others might also want?

Idea 52 – Information sites #2: GuruNet

This is a terrific idea because, apart from anything else, it demonstrates that all the really good ideas on the Net *weren't* taken years ago. This business only launched in late 1999, and it has hit the ground running.

The founders of GuruNet reckoned that it was taking users far too long to hunt for information on the Internet, so they invented a better system – what they call an 'instant expert'. Here's how it works. You download the 750KB free package and you can use it any time you're online. If you want more information about any word on screen you simply point at it, hold down the ALT key and left-click on your mouse. A GuruNet pop-up window appears and gives you information about the word.

This doesn't just mean dictionary, encyclopedia and thesaurus information. If you point on a company name, it can give you a company profile. It also includes weather, news, sports news and stock quotes, and is adding more information all the time. It works by sending your query to an Internet server, which means it can be far more comprehensive than a CD-ROM, and is right up-to-the-minute. It works in any PC application, such as email, MS-Office, PIMs and any browser.

This is a deliciously simple idea, with easy-to-use technology which provides a really useful service – what more can you ask? It's a great example of what a valuable commodity information is on the Web, and how there always seems to be another worthwhile way to deliver it just waiting to be found. Find them on www.guru.net.

Ask yourself

GuruNet was founded on the idea of making Internet users' lives easier. What other services would make the Internet quicker, cheaper or easier to use?

Idea 53 – Information sites #3: Yodlee

Online banking is really taking off these days. In fact, you can pay bills online, check your credit card balance or review your investments. With an array of Web sites, you can do practically anything. Of course, it's not so easy to move money online from one bank account to a separate account with another bank. And you have to go to another Web site to review your mortgage payments. And another to pay off the next instalment of your car loan.

Or do you? This is where Yodlee comes in. It was founded in 1999 on the principle that people don't want to have to move between unintegrated sites to execute financial arrangements and transactions online. It would be far better if everything were accessible at one site, in one view. So now it is.

Yodlee.com delivers the first ever Web Personalisation Platform, as it is termed. A single, secure Web site gives you access to view all your personal accounts across the Web with a single click, using just one password. In partnership with over a thousand popular sites (so far), Yodlee gives its customers an integrated financial package, accessible from your desk or from mobile and wireless devices such as smart phones.

Your customised, personal page summarises all the online activities you tell it to, from banking and investment accounts to travel reservations, store cards, unread emails, online shopping and the like. You can also customise your personal page to give you reminders, news, sport, entertainment information and other non-personal data. And from your Yodlee page you can access your online accounts without having to enter a separate password.

Yodlee is a private company (with some impressive investors), which spotted a weakness in Internet financial services; namely that they were reluctant to integrate for fear of losing control of their own customers. Yodlee has come up with an information package that promises to become increasingly valuable as more and more people do business, bank, and pay household bills online.

Ask yourself

Integration is not, so far, the Web's strong suit. Are there any opportunities to integrate Internet services that you could exploit?

Nine Greatest Ideas for Making Money Without Even Starting a Business

The ideas so far have been great, but if you don't have a business already, most of them aren't much use. You could start a business, of course – but maybe you're happy with your job and you don't want to give up everything to work 16 hours a day with no holidays for the next five years. Perhaps you picked up this book because you wanted to make money on the Internet without turning your life upside down.

OK then. This section should give you want you want. These ideas are all ones that you can use on the side without having to give up the day job. There's a good selection here, from using the Internet to make some regular pocket money (*Ideas 54* and *55*), to selling through the Net without having to freeze at car boot sales (*Ideas 56* and *57*). Or you might try registering a domain name and – if you're smart – you could hit the jackpot (*Idea 60*). If you're looking for something a little more professional, why not use the Web to find yourself a job (*Idea 58*), or to go into business with someone else and let them do all the work (*Idea 59*)? From the dodgy world of hacking to auctioning your old computer on the Net, there are plenty of ways for anyone to make money using the Web.

Idea 54 – Get paid to surf the Net

This is one of those ideas that sounds too good to be true – except that it is true. To be fair, you're not likely to make millions out of it, but it's a decent source of pocket money and it costs you nothing. Or, if you really want to make an effort, you could make a few hundred quid a month from it.

All you do is download a communications window, which sits at the bottom of your screen whenever you're online. This collects information about the sites you visit so as to build up a profile of you and your interests. Using this information, companies advertise their products to you through the communications window.

You get paid monthly according to how long you spend online, up to a maximum of 25 hours. This works out at about $12.50 (the rate can vary), which is converted into your own currency. Not a great deal of money, but better than a kick in the teeth. However, if you refer anyone else to the service, you also get paid for all the time *they* spend surfing. Refer five of your friends, and you could earn as much from them as you do on your own account. (It's not a rake-off, because they still get the full amount too.) And you get paid for anyone they refer and so on. If you really go all out to refer people, you can end up making hundreds (although you have to keep surfing yourself to claim the money).

You can do the maths yourself, but the point is that with no effort you can make something for nothing, and with more effort you can make more money – as much as several hundred a month or more. So if you surf the net anyway, why not check it out? Try www.alladvantage.com.

Idea 55 – Get paid to read your emails

Personally, I hate receiving unsolicited emails, and I would pay someone else money to keep them away from me. But plenty of people are more tolerant than I am, and if you're one of them you might like this idea. It's very similar in principal to *Idea 54*.

You simply get paid to read emails sent to you by advertisers, after indicating what your interests are. The number of emails you receive may be several a day, and will depend on the interests you have ticked. You get a standard rate for each email sent to you and, again, you also get paid for every referral you make. This means that if you have a hundred referrals, you might make something in the region of £20 a day. Once again, you'll never be a millionaire this way, but you might well make a decent amount on the side if you're prepared to make the effort.

If you enjoy reading emails, contact www.sendmoreinfo.com.

Idea 56 – Small ads

If you have something to sell, from an old bed frame or a used PlayStation to a collection of second-hand roof tiles or an early edition of Winnie-the-Pooh, where would you go to sell it? Most of us would either advertise in the local paper, or perhaps a specialist publication, or take it down to a car boot sale and try to flog it.

But why not sell it online? The Internet has around 12 million users in the UK alone – that's got to be a better catchment than the local paper. OK, not all of them will look at your ad, but then neither will everyone who picks up the local freebie. One of the biggest of these online marts is Amazon's zShops, which you can find at www.amazon.co.uk.

You may or may not be charged a basic rate for your listing, and you will have to pay a little extra to have your listing highlighted in bold type. Unlike a newspaper ad, you can include a photograph of the item you're selling. And unlike a car boot or jumble sale, you can sell the item without going out of your front door.

Here's the twist

The final deal is between you and the buyer; the Web site owner is not responsible for the honesty of the buyer. So take all reasonable precautions, such as receiving the money before you part with the goods, just as you would if you were selling through the local paper.

Idea 57 – Going, going … gone

Maybe you like the idea of selling items you have no use for on the Web, but you're not sure what they're worth. You wouldn't want to undercharge, after all. In that case, why not auction them? Online auctions are easy to enter items for, and you simply sit back and wait to see how much they fetch. You stipulate the reserve price, so there's no danger of selling below your minimum price.

There are plenty of auction sites springing up all over the Web, the most famous being eBay, which has a UK site at www.ebay.co.uk. Amazon now has an auction site too, and there are also specialist auction sites, such as www.digibid.com, which sells high-end audio and video equipment, or www.winebid.com, where you can sell vintage wines, and sites such as those in *Idea 61* where you can sell domain names at auction.

Idea 58 – Get on your (virtual) bike

Perhaps your preferred way of making money is through your job. The Internet can still help, by locating the best job for you. There is no shortage of Internet sites to help job-hunters, and many of them offer additional services such as help preparing your CV, or email notification when a job matching your specification comes up.

There are specialist job sites, such as www.citycatering.co.uk, which lists jobs in the catering industry (obviously), and www.callcentremanagers.co.uk, which I'll leave you to work out for yourself. Many other sites have spin-off specialist sites; for example the Monster Board (www.monster.co.uk) has civil service, graduate and nursing sites. And other sites allow you to search their vacancies lists by region, salary and keywords. Many sites encourage you to post your CV so that, while you are looking for an employer, prospective employers can check out employees.

At www.jobhunter.co.uk you can browse the job pages of local papers around the UK, and many of the national papers' sites are among the best on the Net for job seekers. Try the *Guardian* at www.jobsunlimited.co.uk, the *Telegraph* at www.appointments-plus.com, or Associated Newspapers (who own the *Daily Mail*) at www.peoplebank.com.

Also worth checking out are www.jobshark.co.uk, www.jobsite.co.uk, www.jobsearch.co.uk, and www.jobulike.com. and if you secure an interview and want advice on how to handle it, try www.topjobs.co.uk, or www.careermosaic-uk.co.uk.

The jobsearch process on the Web is often rated as being a much more positive experience than trawling the papers. You feel more actively involved, and the feedback – such as daily emails of new listings from sites – gives the whole thing a more personal touch. So if you're not happy with your job, log on and find yourself something better.

Idea 59 – The lazy person's way of setting up in business

Do you have any specialist skill that would be useful in running a business, but don't want to run the whole thing? Maybe you're a marketing specialist, but you can't face managing a business with all that admin, finance and so on to cope with as well. Or perhaps you're a financial whizz, but only want to put a few hours a week into running a small business, not five or six days.

Well, it can be done. All you need is to find a small business that desperately needs marketing skills or financial input or whatever in order to expand. Instead of taking a consultancy fee, you ask for a share in the business. Then when it grows – thanks to you – the value of your share grows with it.

This has a great advantage over paid consultancy, because once your expertise is no longer needed, or at least less input is required of you, you can repeat the exercise with another business, and another, and another … and end up with shares in all of them.

The businesses you choose will, obviously, want to check you out thoroughly. This is not an idea for those with two years experience as a filing clerk, I'm afraid. But if you have plenty of experience, a good track record, and can demonstrate that you can have a significant impact on the company's growth, many small businesses will welcome you with open arms. You can find small businesses in need of expertise through business incubators; organisations that nurse small businesses through their first few months and help them find funding and so on. You'll find plenty of them on the Web if you search for 'business incubators'.

Clearly the greatest skill you need, alongside your own specialism, which you are offering in exchange for shares instead of cash, is the ability to recognise a promising business. But assuming you can recognise a business that has potential and lacks only your input to fulfil it, you're quids in. If you pick the right businesses you can get rich extremely quickly this way. It's a kind of venture capital investment where you invest skills instead of cash.

Ask yourself

Do I have any business skills that are sufficiently valuable to small businesses to be worth exchanging for shares?

Idea 60 – What's in a name?

Back in the mid-1990s, a few smart people realised that the Internet was going to be huge and started registering domain names (in other words, Web site names). They realised that these names would become extremely valuable before long, and they would be sitting on a gold mine. And they were right. It is becoming increasingly hard to find good, catchy, memorable names that aren't already registered, and many businesses will buy an existing name from the owner rather than think up a less memorable name that is free to be registered.

Some of these domain names can become immensely valuable: bingo.com was sold for $1m, and business.com for a whopping $7.5m. It is generally considered rather bad form to register domain names simply for the sake of selling them later at a profit, but plenty of people are doing it. There aren't many names left that are worth millions, but plenty of names will be worth tens of thousands. The rule used to be that domain names were limited to 23 characters. However, in December 1999 this rule was changed to allow names up to 67 characters long. This opened up a whole new gold rush of domain name registrations.

You can register a domain name (or as many as you like) for about $60 US each (the rate varies according to where you register it) for two years, with first refusal to renew after that time. Go to a site such as www.greatdomains.com, www.register.com, or www.igoldrush.com. These sites will all allow you to search to find out if the name you want is still available, and then to register your name once you have found one that is free. However, there are certain ground rules you need to follow to choose the most profitable names to register:

- The more types of business that might use your name, the more valuable it is. That's why business.com was worth so much. A name such as gardentools.com is worth much less, although obviously to a garden tool company it would still be valuable.
- Simple words which don't limit the nature of the business, and which are easily branded, are also valuable. Amazon.com is a good example of this.
- Well-known phrases, such as wakeupandsmellthecoffee.com, can attract good traffic to a site and therefore be valuable.
- The fewer characters your domain name has, the more valuable it is
- Domain names ending .com are worth about four times more than names which end .net, and about ten times more than any other endings such as .org or .co.uk.

- Names that have plenty of keywords that search engines will pick up on are valuable, and search engines love hyphens. So you could register phone-fax-computer-goods, for example. It is often worthwhile, if you do this, registering the non-hyphenated version too, since people prefer using these.

Forget cybersquatting

There was a time when some people thought it would be clever to register companies' brand names before they registered them themselves, and then selling the name back to the company for a small fortune. If you owned coca-cola.com, for example, you could flog it to the real Coca-Cola for a pretty penny. However, it doesn't work.

Big companies who find their names taken by gold diggers are now pursuing them in court, and winning the right to have their names back. The people who registered the names not only lose the name, but often pay thousands in court costs too. In the US, companies can claim damages of up to $100,000 against anyone else registering their name.

What is less clear is the position of small businesses that genuinely have the same name as a larger corporation. For example, if you run a rural dairy that has been in the family for a hundred and fifty years and is named after your great-grandfather, JP Morgan, can you set up a Web site with the domain name JP Morgan? All I can tell you is that if you are in this position, I think you should seek legal advice.

While cybersquatting, as it is known, is definitely not permitted, there are some interesting grey areas that have not yet been legally tested. One of these is known as typosquatting (yes, really). For example, if you want to go to Amazon's online bookstore but accidentally key in amazom.com, it will take you to a rival bookstore run by Books.com, who then display a disclaimer stating that they are not in any way connected with amazon.com.

Both domain name registrations and metatag keywords (see *Idea 41*) have been used to help divert customers away from competitors, and the first trial cases are under way. For example, one perfume company took out an advertising arrangement with certain search engines, which meant that if anyone searched for Estée Lauder, the banner advertisement immediately displayed the rival company's ad. Another ruse, which the courts generally frown on, is putting other companies' names in your metatag. However one former Playboy Playmate of the Year was allowed by the courts to tag her site using the magazine's name.

Selling your domain name

Once you have registered a domain name that you reckon is worth something, what do you do with it? You could just sit back and wait for someone to approach you (via the central register that holds your contact details). Or you could advertise it for sale. The Web sites listed above where you can register your domain name – and others like them – also sell names, through straight advertising or at online auction. They generally list your name for free, and charge a commission if it sells. Most of them also offer a valuation service, since you probably won't have a clue how much to ask.

Even if a domain name makes as little as a thousand pounds, it will turn a profit. And there's satisfaction in knowing that the money you make is largely down to your own ingenuity in thinking up valuable names that no one else has thought of first.

> Who steals my purse steals trash; 'tis something, nothing;
> 'Twas mine, 'tis his, and has been slave to thousands;
> But he that filches from me my good name
> Robs me of that which not enriches him,
> And makes me poor indeed.
>
> William Shakespeare, *Othello*

Idea 61 – The spin of the wheel

It is possible to get really lucky and make a fortune through online casino gambling, just as it is possible to get lucky and find £100,000 in used notes just lying in the street. But whatever anybody tells you, there is absolutely *no* system that will leave you odds on to make a fortune, let alone guarantee it. The only sure-fire way to make money out of gambling is to own the casino.

Ask yourself

Just how big a sucker am I?

Idea 62 – The devil in the machine

Unfortunately, despite the numerous great ways to make money on the Internet, some people choose to use illegal methods instead. One of the most lucrative of these is hacking. Many hackers have non-financial motives such as getting back at former employers, or huge corporations that they feel represent the worst aspects of capitalism.

Many others, however, use their technological expertise to steal software or credit card details; one of the most famous of these cyber criminals is Kevin Mitnick, who started his career proper by stealing $1 million worth of software from a company in Silicon Valley. After a year inside for this crime, he emerged an unchanged man. He used a complicated system to exploit a (then) loophole in the Internet and steal twenty thousand credit card numbers.

Groups of hackers known as cyberterrorists have blackmailed big financial institutions, threatening to destroy their computer systems unless several million dollars are paid into offshore accounts; these hackers demonstrate their seriousness by damaging the system before demanding the payoff. Several organisations have paid the money rather than risk the collapse of their system.

Many of the most serious instances of hacking have led to a tightening of the system, making it harder and harder to break into. But inevitably the most skilled hackers will always find a way to get one step ahead.

Eight Greatest Ideas for Small Businesses on the Internet

If you're already running a small business, you may have reached the stage where you realise that you need an Internet presence. And if you're not there yet, you almost certainly will be soon. It is becoming increasingly important to have your own Web site, simply because everyone else is doing it. If you're not on the Web, with a Web site address printed on your letterheads and comp slips alongside your phone and fax numbers, it gives you the image of being less than professional, up-to-date and able to give a fast service. Unfair maybe, but that's beside the point.

Making the transition from terra firma to cyberspace can seem pretty scary, especially if you don't feel you're that computer literate to begin with. But it has to be done. So grit your teeth, and follow these great ideas for making the best of it, from getting online (*Ideas 63* and *64*) to making the most of it once you're there.

There's a huge difference between having a Web site and really making money from it, so follow some of the other ideas here (and in the next section) to make your site more profitable. Simple things like counting your visitors and keeping your site up to date (*Ideas 65* and *66*) will make a big difference, and then there are various ways of increasing traffic to your site via other Web sites (*Idea 67*), or simply via the press in the old fashioned way (*Idea 68*). It's not only your own Web site that will help you earn money; once you're online you can even get a better deal from your bank (*Idea 70*).

You simply need to be online to start opening up possibilities for expanding your business. There's no excuse for not doing it; it can only boost your business, so long as you do it right. Before long you'll be a thoroughgoing nettie, and you'll wonder how you ever managed in the old days.

Idea 63 – Create your cybershop front

It really isn't difficult to set up your own Web site, and it is becoming increasingly essential for almost every business. Once your customers expect you to have a Web site, you really have to do it. If that's how they want to place their orders, check your current prices or remind themselves of the colourways or sizes available for a particular product, you'd better make sure they have the option. And as more and more people join the Web, so the pressure mounts to be there yourself.

You can assemble a serviceable Web site in as little as an hour. There are plenty of online services that guide you through the process, so you can create your own design. You also need to buy webspace from a web hosting company, which varies in price according to how much space you need, but can be as little as £15 a month. You will have to work out how many web pages you want, as this will be a deciding factor in how much space you need. You can plan what pages you will need by taking a pen and paper and mapping out a flowchart showing which pages lead where, and what the content of each is.

You will also need to decide whether you should offer ordering facilities online – this is easy to do through many of the simplest packages available, and many Internet users say that they really want to be able to order online. If you think your customers want this facility, provide it. Better still, don't guess – ask them.

If you want to build your own Web site, try visiting www.zy.com, www.ibm.com/hpc or www.webtoolpro.com.

Idea 64 – Naming names

When customers and prospects want to visit your site, they will have to key in your Web site address, or URL (Uniform Resource Locator). They may not always have it written down in front of them, however, so you need a URL that is easily memorable, and preferably related to your business name or your product.

The guidelines for registering domain names (*Idea 60*) are useful here; if your own name is well known you will probably want to use it. But if you want to attract visitors who may not know or remember your name, you can choose a completely different one for your Web site address. In this case, you need a name that is catchy, stands out from the rest, and relates to your product or service.

Suppose your business name is HP Wilkins, and you sell office stationery. Instead of using hpwilkins as your Web site address, you could choose something completely different. How about paperandstaples.com, for example? Generally speaking, people who can't quite remember your name will guess at it, so you might also register staplesandpaper.com and have it redirected to your Web site (see *Idea 25*). For the same reason, you're best off with a .com ending, since this is what people tend to try first. In the UK, your next best bets are .net and .co.uk.

It will cost you a few quid to register your own domain name but it's worth it. There are free services around which will give you an address which consists of *their* domain name, followed by a forward slash, followed by your own name. This really isn't worth the thirty or forty pounds it saves you, because it looks less professional, makes you look like a business that can't afford to survive without cutting corners, and gives you a less memorable Web site address.

Here's the twist

So many domain names have already been registered that the one you want may not be available. You may have to run down through a list of options before you find one that you can register. So prepare a list of choices and put them in order.

Idea 65 – Keep counting

You need to know how many people are visiting your site, since this is your best way of knowing how successful it is, and how successful your promotions are. Suppose your visitor rate goes up but the number of online enquiries and orders stays the same – this should alert you that something is wrong somewhere. Suppose a certain promotion increases the number of visitors – how will you know? Suppose the visitor rate starts to tail off – if you don't know, how can you do anything about it?

Use a reliable method of counting; some systems will also track visitor activity once they are inside your site. Try www.accipiter.com, www.netcount.com, or www.webtrends.com.

Idea 66 – Keep on top of your revision

Once your Web site is up and running, it's no good just leaving it alone. You may not be able to afford a permanent member of staff assigned to it, but you must allocate regular time to keeping it up-to-date. For a start that means you need to make sure all the information on it is correct: update price lists and product profiles, delete discontinued lines, mention special offers and so on.

But there's more to it than that if you want your Web site to be profitable. You need to make sure that it's the site your visitors want it to be. Using a visitor-tracking program, you can check which pages your visitors do and don't visit, and what they do when they are there. This means you can find out if you need to remove or replace certain pages, or if it seems that your visitors want one area of the site expanded.

For example, suppose your office stationery site includes an information page, explaining paper sizes and materials, what to look for if you want to buy eco-friendly office products, industry statistics on how many letterheads the average company mails out each day and so on – items of interest or use to the average buyer. If this page is visited frequently, that suggests that your customers and prospects like it. So it stands to reason that if you expand the page and keep it regularly refreshed with new data, your visitors will be pleased. They will be more likely to visit your site and recommend it to others, and will value you more as a supplier. Now that has to be good business.

You don't have to rely on traffic analysis programs. You can always ask your visitors what they want more or less of (see *Idea 27*). They will generally be happy to tell you, since it means they will get the Web site they want from you. And of course you can ask them offline too, either by talking to individual customers or by sending out a survey form in the post or with each delivery. As with all customer surveys, it is important that you take action as a result, or they will wonder why they bothered to answer your questions. Ideally, post a summary of the survey results on your Web site and explain what changes you are making as a result.

We haven't the money, so we've got to think.

Lord Rutherford

Ask yourself

What can we do to make our site interesting and helpful not only to visit but also to revisit?

Idea 67 – Get into bed with the big boys

In *Idea 33* I talked about setting up an affiliate program, whereby another site carries your link, and you pay them a commission for every click-through, or every sale generated via a click-through. But you can do this the other way round, too. You can carry links for other sites, and charge a commission for visitors they attract via your site.

This has two advantages. Firstly, you will obviously earn commission from your Web site, assuming any of your visitors click on the links. But secondly, you can use the technique to build credibility with your visitors. The link associates you with the organisation it links to, so pick businesses with a good reputation. If your stationery information page offers links to the top computer equipment suppliers, for example, that's a useful service, should earn you some commission, and also makes you seem important by association. How can you lose?

Your best approach is to think of the businesses you would most like to offer links to or carry ads for. Then visit their Web sites. If they don't run an affiliate program already, contact them to ask if they would like to set up an arrangement. They can't lose if it's on a commission basis – from their point of view, if you have very few visitors by their standards, they will only have to pay out a small commission; whatever happens, they only pay for what they get.

Ask yourself

What non-competing industry giants would we like to associate ourselves with?

Idea 68 – Tell your story

Just because you're on the Net, it doesn't mean that the rest of the old world doesn't exist any more. You can use the local and trade press to promote your Web site, as well as using online ezines (see *Idea 36*). Going online can make a good story in itself if you are in certain businesses – maybe you've started selling funerals online, or vintage typewriters – you might even make the national press.

If your customers are mostly local, then local press coverage is all you need. Find an interesting angle on the story, coupled with a good photo (not just a mugshot), and the local press should do a lot of your publicity for you.

Ask yourself

How can we make the story of our business going online appealing to the press? What angle would make it sound different from every other business that is going online?

Idea 69 – Look who's talking

One very simple technique for encouraging visitors to your Web site is hosting a chat. You can download the necessary software from the Web, and then hold a real-time chat. In other words, people who join the chat can type messages to each other that can be read as they are being typed. 'Talk' software enables two people to communicate in this way; 'chat' software enables groups to communicate in real time.

Keeping a chat line constantly open doesn't work unless you have tens of thousands of customers you can invite to join in. But as a small business, holding chat events is a useful way to encourage visitors to your Web site. You need to promote the event both on and offline, and hold a chat for, say, a specific two hours, which you publicise.

Among the most popular chat events are those involving celebrities (no surprises there). So if you sell yachting equipment, for example, invite your customers to an online chat with a famous round-the-world yachtsperson. Another possibility is to invite a politician to participate in a chat about impending legislation that will affect your customers. Or you could host an event in which your customers talk to each other about a subject of interest to them all. You can function as a central monitor to make sure things stay pleasant (if necessary), and on the subject.

Ask yourself

What might our Web site visitors be interested in chatting about which we could facilitate?

Idea 70 – Steal a march

Here's an idea which may be of particular use to small businesses, and which doesn't involve your Web site at all. It simply requires you to be online. If you are, you can use online banking, which is fast making queueing down at the high street bank seem like a mug's game.

Among the many, many advantages of online banking is the fact that you can pay bills and move money between your accounts at any hour of the day or night. And it's very simple for a small business to make money out of this. How often do you have large sums of money arriving in your current account and sitting there for a few days before they either get paid out again, or transferred to a high interest account when you get the chance?

With online banking, you can transfer these sums to your high interest account the day they clear, and back again two days later if you need to. Or simply transfer them a couple of days before you would have got round to it otherwise. I don't know what kind of sums you deal in, but you can work the figures out for yourself. Suppose you have £10,000 in a high interest account paying, say, 5% interest. That would earn you well over a pound a day. So if you transferred it 48 hours earlier than you would have done otherwise, that's over £2.50.

I know £2.50 doesn't sound like a whole lot, but imagine you do this regularly – every time you get a large payment you get it transferred to a high interest earning account two days early. Or transferred for a week before you transfer it back and pay it all out again. Over the course of a year you're looking at several hundred pounds which you wouldn't have had otherwise.

The point about online banking is not that you can't do this down at your local high street branch; it's that you don't have time. But with online banking you can simply make it the last job of the day, after everyone else has gone home and you've got five minutes to yourself, to check your finances and see if you can benefit from moving money around your accounts. It takes only two or three minutes, and it could make you hundreds of pounds a year.

Ask yourself

Are we really making the most of our money, or could we get more out of our bank if everything was at our fingertips?

Eleven Greatest Ideas for Designing a Profitable Web Site

You must have visited Web sites which you have thought were dreadful, and never gone back. Sometimes they just don't have the information you want, but often you never get that far because the design is so atrocious. Maybe you can't find your way around, or perhaps the information you need isn't there. Perhaps it takes so long to order that you've fallen asleep before you're halfway through the process – or perhaps you've looked at the products, decided what you want, and then discovered that you're not actually allowed to order online at all. You have to phone up to do that.

It's embarrassing how many Web sites make these kinds of mistakes. They aren't just missing out on business; they are frustrating and alienating their customers, and making them reluctant to come back, or determined not to.

The difference, in terms of profit, between a poorly designed Web site and a well-designed one can be huge. Many specialists reckon that the average value of each lost customer can be thousands of pounds over a few years. Assuming you know how much each of your existing customers is worth to you, you should be able to see how damaging an off-putting Web site is.

Not only that, but encouraging customers to deal with you online makes sense. A well-designed Web site, with automated ordering facilities, can handle information requests, orders, order queries and offer alternatives when products are out of stock or discontinued (see *Idea 15*). Think of how much staff time that could free up. If everyone communicated with you over the Web there'd be no more checking up on orders, no more order taking, no more taking down addresses for brochure mailings, no more answering price and delivery time queries … think of all the staff time you'd free up to concentrate on both online and offline promotion.

You presumably want to make sure that your Web site is recognising its full potential, not leaving your customers fed up and irritated. It is a basic rule of business etiquette to remember that your customers are paying to be online, so don't waste their time. So here are the best ideas for making the design of your Web site friendly, fun and easy for your visitors to use.

Idea 71 – Time is of the essence

The first frustrating problem that visitors can encounter is a home page that takes forever to load. They key in your Web site address, and five minutes later they are still waiting for your home page to appear on the screen. Or, having reached your home page, it takes ages to open any other pages. This is enough to deter many people from using your site at all, or at least they will decide not to bother visiting your special offers page, or your 'what's new' page. One research company has found that if a page won't load within eight seconds, the odds are that visitors will abort the process and go to another site.

As a general rule of thumb, try to keep page sizes under 30K, and don't allow images to get too big; 15K is a good maximum to set. Remember, many of your visitors may use a fairly slow connection, so this is plenty big enough. Take into account the time of day when you get most visits, too. If you attract home users to your site, they will tend to log on after work and at weekends when the Internet is at its busiest and therefore running quite slow enough already.

And remember the three-click rule, which states that people are likely to give up looking for information if it takes more than three clicks to get to it from your home page. So aim for a Web site that is broad rather than deep.

Ask yourself

How long am I prepared to wait for the home page to load on other people's sites before I start to get frustrated?

Idea 72 – Take me home

Your site may be very complicated to navigate around for someone who is new to it and who can arrive via a search engine on any page, not necessarily your home page. Just because you know your way around easily, don't assume everyone else does. One of the most important things you can do to help with this is to provide a 'return to home page' link on every page, and a clear contents on the home page for when the visitor gets there.

Idea 73 – Don't get smart

One of the most common mistakes that businesses make with their Web site design is trying to look clever. Visitors want a quick and easy journey through your site, during which they can find everything they want in whatever order they want it. Period.

Cluttered pages, fancy designs, Java applets, large designs that take forever to load – none of these will impress your customers half so much as a clear, simple navigator bar, or a page that fits on the screen without having to scroll across. In fact, many of these will irritate your customers, especially if they don't have the latest technology to support them.

There's plenty of research going on that is finding that these kinds of frustrations deter huge numbers of potential customers from buying. And remember that your online and offline activities are all part of the same service in your customers' eyes. Poor service is poor service, and the whole of your organisation will be tarred with the Internet brush.

Idea 74 – Follow the Web page rules

You may have noticed that Web pages don't look like printed pages. That's because it's pretty hard to read a great chunk of unbroken text on screen. It never hurts to assume that your visitors have the attention span of a goldfish; even those of us capable of lengthy periods of concentration offline somehow lose the skill entirely once we log on.

So present information in small chunks, where visitors can find and read it in moments. If your site calls for longer passages of text, provide clear links so that visitors can find it easily if they want it. Use plenty of clearly indicated hyperlinks so that, if you refer to information elsewhere on your site, a simple click will take the user there.

You can't assume that once they reach any given page your users will necessarily read the whole page. So put the most important information at the top. For example, if you have a special offers page, make sure the offers you most want to promote are at the top of the page.

You'll need to consider the size of your pages, too. Plenty of people are still using old technology, with a screen size of 640 × 480 pixels, so generally speaking you should design to suit this. The exception is if you know that your customers all have the latest technology – perhaps they are all City firms, or software designers.

Idea 75 – Making contact

Many of your visitors will want to make contact with you after they've viewed your Web site. Perhaps they can't find the information they want, or they have a query about an order, or they want to comment on your site (and you want all the free market research you can get). So have a clear 'contact us' button on your navigation bar, or at least on your home page.

Once a visitor clicks on the 'contact us' button, you should offer them every possible method of contact. They are most likely, as Web users, to want to email you, and you should provide a link for them to do this. But give them phone and fax numbers too, and a physical mailing address. Quite apart from the fact that they may want to use it, a physical address gives you credibility. Businesses that don't want to tell their customers where they are based can be dodgy businesses, and your users know this.

If customers choose to email you, make sure you respond promptly. If you can't give a full reply immediately, have a system that sends an email acknowledging their message, and telling them when they can expect a full response from you. This buys you some time, but it doesn't make it OK to say you will reply on Wednesday fortnight. Aim to reply within 48 hours at the most, unless you cannot get hold of the information they want that quickly, in which case tell them so.

Idea 76 – Be a show-off

When your customers walk into your showroom, or the retail outlet that stocks your products, they can pick things up, feel them, turn them around, see what happens when they drop them, and generally interact with them.

They can't, of course, do this at your Web site. So you need to give them all the help you can. Show them the back view as well as the front, include an inset close-up of the material itself, show all the colourways in full, show the item both folded up and fully extended … whatever you think your customers might need to see in order to be confident enough to place an order.

You can even use the latest technology to animate your products; spin them so that the viewer can see them from all sides, or open and close them. This can be expensive if you have to use a special camera, but it can more than pay off in increased sales in some lines of business. Be inventive about how you can show off your products. Some American baseball stadiums help to sell tickets by showing the view from different seats on their Web site.

Here's the twist

How many products should you show to a page? Apparently, products on a second or third page attract around 50 per cent fewer orders, because so many visitors never get that far. So you need to design a site that doesn't require visitors to go too deep; break your products down into smaller groups, and fit all the items in each group onto a single page, with a 'click here for more info' button by each product.

Idea 77 – Place an order? No problem

It's a funny thing, but when you ask Internet users what they want from a good Web site, the majority of them say they want to be able to order online. And yet a high proportion of Web sites offer no more than a glorified brochure (or even an unglorified one). Some research studies have shown that for the average company, over half the orders that have been placed online are permanently lost if there isn't an ordering option.

So if customers want to order online, you'd better let them. OK, it means arranging credit and debit card facilities, and setting up an ordering system, but the cost is minimal. And you could pick up a lot more orders. For one thing, customers who go to all the trouble of visiting your Web site and looking at your products, only to find that they can't order them, are likely to be very irritated – which may well deter them from ordering at all. And for another thing, the Internet is a great way to pick up impulse orders. By the time the visitor has written down the phone or fax number and logged off, they may have changed their mind.

Of course, there are a few businesses where customers are unlikely to order online. If you sell aircraft carriers or luxury country houses your customers will probably want to talk to you before they place an order. But you might be surprised at what people will buy without any other form of contact, assuming your Web site is well designed and tells them everything they want to know. For the vast majority of businesses, online ordering is vital.

Make it easy

Once you have made the decision to include an ordering facility (well done), you still need to think about the process. Many Web sites commit the most crass mistakes, such as forgetting to include a checkout button to allow visitors to complete their order. But even if the system works, it still needs to be easy and flexible. Check out other sites to see what works well and what doesn't, but here are a few basic rules:

- Make it straightforward for customers to go back, at any stage of the ordering process, and add an item they had forgotten
- Don't make people fill in endless forms with contact details. Once they've written them once, give them a box to tick to copy them to the despatch address (assuming it's the same).
- Give existing customers a password, or use their name and postcode, to save them having to repeat contact details which they have given you in the past.
- Allow customers who already know your product line to go straight to a fast ordering service, without having to wade through your catalogue first.

- Let customers access information (via a password) about their past orders, so they can check what it was they ordered before, or how many they usually have, in order to place this order.

Here's the twist

You'll need to automate your ordering system, of course (see *Idea 8*), or you'll waste a lot of staff time processing orders when they could be promoting products.

Idea 78 – How do I know I can trust you?

One of the biggest difficulties in persuading people to order products on the Net is that they don't feel safe giving out their credit card details over the Web. This fear is not entirely rational, since it is arguably just as risky giving it to a mail-order company over the phone, but it is a very real fear, and you need to recognise it. Most people are only happy – if at all – if you use a secure payment system. This is very simple to set up through a secure server.

However, it is possible that some of your customers may be using a browser that does not support secure servers. If you think this is likely, you have two options, and ideally you should use both (plus the secure server for those who are able to use it):

- Give them an order form that they can print out and then either mail or fax to you.

- Give them an online order form, but invite them either to include a credit card number if they wish, or to leave this blank and you will phone them for it.

You *can* set up a system whereby customers order online via a 'transaction company' that handles the secure ordering for you. They require the customer to set up an account number and password with them in order to take the order. But apart from the hassle for the customer – who may well just give up on the whole thing – the other problem to look out for here is the time the transaction companies take to pay you the money they collect for you. It typically takes at least 21 days, and sometimes as many as 90, for the money to reach you.

Idea 79 – Keeping tabs

Once your customer has placed their order, they may feel slightly in the dark about it. For some reason, the order seems somehow less concrete when you haven't placed it with a real person. So, despite the email confirmation of the order, which you should send within hours, you should also include order tracking on your site.

This program allows visitors to see – generally by keying in an order number you have given them – exactly what is happening to their order. Is it waiting for new stock, being packaged or already on its way to them? Order tracking gives customers confidence that their order is being processed, as well as telling them where it is. If the delivery is overdue, many customers will check it online and save your operators having to deal with the query.

You can, of course, use online order tracking to check up on orders that were placed by phone, fax or post. This is a valuable service for customers who are on the Web but choose not to order from you online. And, once in your site, they may decide to order online in future – which frees up your staff time.

Ask yourself

What information could we give our customers online that would both make their lives easier and take the pressure off our telesales or customer services people?

Idea 80 – Come clean

In *Idea 26* I mentioned cookies, which track a visitor's movements and are often used to target suitable advertising at them. Many Web users, however, understandably don't like cookies as they feel they are being spied on. In fact, many users tell their browser not to accept cookies.

Some sites are set up so that they need to use cookies; these sites are missing out on all the customers who have chosen the 'disable cookies' option. So clearly you should avoid the kind of system that means that your site has to use cookies. But even without having to use them, many sites give cookies to all visitors who will accept them. These visitors don't know that they are being given a cookie – unless you tell them.

By far the best policy, assuming you use cookies, is to be honest about it. Building credibility is an essential part of creating a profitable Web site, since most of the reluctance to do business over the Web is due to the fact that people are wary and untrusting of it, since it is all too easy to remain anonymous, take their money and then vanish into cyberspace. Coming clean about cookies is not only the fairest approach, it also helps convince users that you are reliable and honest.

So if you use cookies:

- Tell visitors that you are about to give them a cookie.
- Explain what a cookie is for those that don't know.
- State what information you will collect, and what you will do with it.
- Tell them they don't have to accept the cookie.
- Explain clearly how they can prevent their browser accepting cookies.

Idea 81 – Testing, testing, 1,2,3

Once you have designed your site to be as profitable as possible, you must test it. That doesn't just mean spending a few minutes running through it – it means testing thoroughly. Any omission or flaw in the system could cost you sales, so take testing seriously.

Testing a large-scale commercial site should take you at least a month. We already looked at usability testing in *Idea 27*, but you will obviously test the site yourself as well as getting others to help. The key rule of site testing is that once you start testing, you must stop developing the site, otherwise you are wasting your time. Once you have completed the testing, you can repair or improve the problems that it has shown up, but if you develop the site further you must start testing all over again.

As well as usability testing, the key things to test are:

- the ordering process from start to finish, including what happens if a customer changes their mind, wants to add to the quantities at the last minute and so on;
- automated email response times;

- credit card verification and automated billing;
- the effect of the site on your accounts, order fulfilment and despatch departments, and the rest of your organisation's processes such as call centres and sales; and
- simulate heavy traffic to test your servers under pressure.

Ask yourself

What could possibly go wrong with the system? What might customers want to do that we haven't already thought of? What routes might a user take around the site that we haven't considered?

Four Greatest Ideas for Making Money on the Stock Market

Once upon a time, playing the stock markets was something only professionals, fools and the stinking rich did. But suddenly, everyone seems to be doing it, and plenty of them seem to be making a fortune at it, Warren Buffet style. Mind you, an awful lot of others seem to be losing everything.

Only a few years ago, there was no such thing as Internet trading. By 2002 there are likely to be around 14 million online accounts worldwide, holding assets approaching $700 billion. It can cost less than $10 to trade, and many people find it irresistible. All it takes is a little capital and a few clicks. Many people, especially in the US, have given up their day jobs and regard Internet trading as their work.

So is it worth it? The temptations can seem great – who wouldn't want to make enough money to retire on without having to leave home for it? The trouble is, if you're not an expert, it can be difficult knowing how to approach it. How do you know what to buy, or when to sell? What are the best tactics for increasing your investment?

I wouldn't want to give you the impression that the ideas here contain everything you need to know to be a successful online trader. They don't. But they certainly contain many of the most critical guidelines that you need to know before you start, from choosing the best online broker (*Idea 82*) to the vital skill of diversification (*Idea 84*).

Idea 82 – Choose the best broker

Online deals are done through online brokers, obviously. But which broker should you use? There are dozens and dozens, and choosing between them isn't easy. Apart from anything else, it depends what you're after:

- Fast and frequent trading calls for an inexpensive broker, and ideally one with quick Web site navigation and fast trade execution.
- Medium-term investors generally like to do their own research, and often buy into special categories of investment. In this case you need a broker with good research facilities and a comprehensive analysis service.
- Long-term investing, such as investing for retirement, needs a broker with a wide range of options including low risk, steady growth investments.

There are Web sites that can help you choose, such as www.scorecard.com, which scores online brokers and ranks them overall, or by categories such as ease of use, on-site resources and so on. Once you've started to narrow down the field, here are a few key points to check before you make your choice:

- How does the broker compile your tax reports? What you want is a detailed account history, and profit and loss by security.
- If you are planning to day trade, you need to check what backup the broker has for trading if its Internet connection fails, or its server is very busy. Can you trade by phone, for example?
- What interest will your uninvested funds earn? If you make a sale, you probably won't reinvest the money instantly. Some brokers put this money into an interest-earning money-market account, others don't. Of those that do, some do it daily while others do it only weekly.
- What is the price per trade? Although some brokers quote a basic rate of, say, $10, they may charge more for services such as research, making large trades or real-time stock price quotes.

Idea 83 – All in a day's work

The Internet has opened up the possibilities for day trading – buying and selling dozens of different stocks a day, sometimes owning them for as little as a few seconds – to people who had never had the chance before. You can trade before breakfast, in your lunch break and when you get home from work. You may even be able to get away with it sitting at your desk.

There are two main reasons for this surge in day trading:

1 The Web can give you completely up-to-date information, with real-time stock quotes and the ability to buy and sell in moments at the click of a mouse. And it can give you all sorts of data for researching companies, too.
2 Online brokers charge very little to broker deals – often under $10 – which means the likes of us can afford to trade many times in a day. This goes right against the received wisdom that it is better to buy stocks to hold on to.

Who are the day traders? Until very recently they were, typically, educated men, aged between about 30 and 40, with a salary of about £40,000. But recently the profile has broadened widely, to take in teenagers, housewives and retired people, as well as employees looking for a way out of whatever jobs they're in.

If you're going to try to make your fortune in day trading, you'll need nerves of steel, and the ability to think on your feet. Hesitating for a few seconds over a deal can cost you money – so no dithering. And if you really want to make enough money to retire on, follow the golden rules:

- Do your research. Successful day traders spend hours researching companies and scouring the financial pages. Make sure you really know what you're doing before you begin.
- Understand the market. This applies especially if you are day trading for technology stocks. The sector is highly volatile, and while you can make a killing, you can also lose thousands in the time it takes to execute the deal.
- Diversify (see *Idea 84*).
- Don't trade with money you can't afford (*Idea 85*).

- If the bottom starts to drop out of the market, turn off your computer. In other words, when you know you're in a hole, stop digging.

Idea 84 – Diversify

The golden rule of investing of any kind, from long-term strategic investing to day trading, is to diversify. The more diverse your investments, the stronger your safety net, and the more certain your overall growth. Of course there will be times when you think, with hindsight, 'If I'd had all my funds invested in X stocks, I'd be a multimillionaire by now.' But in fact there's every chance you would have had them invested in Y stocks instead, and you'd now be bankrupt. If that's really your style, forget the stock markets, just go to the nearest casino and put everything you've got on red.

What you need to recognise, of course, is that it is inevitable that you will lose money from time to time. Diversification softens the blow. Diversifying doesn't mean simply investing in ten different stocks. It means dividing your portfolio between different kinds of investment, including high-risk ones such as technology stocks and junk bonds, and low-risk ones such as government bonds and money market funds.

Here's the twist

Whilst diversification is the wise approach, you can go too far. Over-diversification dilutes the benefits of diversifying so that the value of your overall investments tends to drift towards the market average, although your risk level doesn't reduce. If the whole market goes into decline, so will you.

Idea 85 – In cyberspace, no one can hear you scream

You read about people who have lost everything trading on the Internet, but there is simply no excuse for this. If you have serious responsibilities – children, a mortgage and so on – and you feel you have the mentality to become a hardened gambler, my best advice is to avoid Internet trading altogether.

Many people liken online trading to casino gambling; you can win and lose high sums of money, and the more you lose the harder you gamble to try and get back on top. It can be addictive for some people. If you have nothing to begin with, and no responsibilities, then you might as well give it a go. But if it's likely to lead to serious trouble, do yourself a favour and don't start.

For those who don't have an addictive personality, it is a much safer way of making money. Even so, it can be tempting in the heat of the moment to invest money you hadn't meant to. Apart from anything else, it seems so innocuous at the time. It's only a few clicks of the mouse, after all. But those few clicks can cost you your house, your children's school fees or your comfortable retirement.

I don't mean to depress you thoroughly. There is a simple way of avoiding this, which works for all but the most addictive of us. It seems obvious, but it can't be that obvious because far too many people don't do it. However, all it needs are a few clear ground rules that you accept as being absolute, and which you must be able to trust yourself to stick to:

- Invest only a small portion – say three to five per cent – of your portfolio in high-risk stocks.
- Make a list of monies that you absolutely will not risk, and stick to it. This might include retirement savings, money set aside to pay your tax bill, money for school fees, money to pay off your car and so on.
- It's not a bad rule to make a deal with yourself that you can reinvest your original 'stake' if you want to, but you won't put any new money into the markets.

It's a bit like going round a penny arcade as a child; your parents gave you a certain amount to start with (if you were lucky), and told you 'When it's all gone, that's it.'

- You can program your account to sell stocks automatically if they drop more than, say, five per cent below your buy-in price.
- *Never* borrow money to invest in the market.

Ask yourself

If everything goes wrong, how much can I afford to lose? This is the absolute maximum you should consider investing.

Two Greatest Ideas for Billing over the Internet

When it comes to charging customers for goods and services, the Internet is – as always – a source of new ideas. From adding customer service value (*Idea 86*) to finding new ways to charge for goods (*Idea 87*), don't assume that you have to keep doing it the way it has always been done in the past. The new technology is providing solutions to all sorts of billing problems, including the problem of persuading people to give out credit card details over the phone. Here are just two examples of what the new technology can do.

Idea 86 – Who needs a bill made of paper?

Isn't it interesting that, although we can now buy and sell online, communicate – even in real time – on the Net, and find information fed into cyberspace by someone on the other side of the world, nevertheless almost all our bills still arrive through the letterbox? Online banking is growing in popularity (see *Idea 70*), making it simple to pay bills online, so why can't they arrive online?

Well, now they can. With automatic bill presentment (sorry about the mouthful, but that's what it's called), suppliers can now send bills to their customers over the Internet. What happens is that if you are the supplier, you make an arrangement with a bill presentment consolidator (sorry again), and the consolidator links to your customer's bank. When your customer starts an online banking session, they will be told that bills are waiting. They open your bill, which gives them transaction information and bill details. You can even enclose promotional information too if you like. And the whole bill carries your brand, as though it had come direct from you.

Once this starts to take off, the convenience of it will become even more obvious, as your customer will be receiving bills online from other suppliers too. In time, householders who bank online will be able to receive bills from utility companies over the Net, making it easy to pay phone, gas, water and electricity bills online.

Ask yourself

Would our customers prefer the convenience of being billed online?

Idea 87 – Charge it to my phone bill

Here's an idea that originated – like so many on the Net – with the porn sites. Many of these adult sites found that visitors were not surprisingly unwilling to give credit card details over the phone. They weren't sure they could trust the kind of people who ran porn sites to be responsible with their money, and perhaps they were worried that their partner might look through the credit card statement and get suspicious.

This posed a big problem for many porn sites, and here's the idea they came up with. When a new subscriber joins the site, they have to download an applet. This application means that whenever the subscriber logs on to the Web site, the applet redials the site through a premium line. So services are free otherwise, and the subscriber simply pays for the time they spend at the site at a premium rate.

Just because the porn sites dreamt up this idea, doesn't mean that no one else can use it. There are many Web sites that could charge users in this way. Suppose you carry a subscription-only newsletter on your site, and have difficulty persuading customers to buy subscriptions over the Net. Or perhaps you charge for access to listings or research material. For all sorts of Internet businesses, this is an alternative if you find visitors are reluctant to give out credit card details over the phone.

Eight Greatest Ideas for Saving Money on the Internet

Saving money may not be worth millions, but it can be worth thousands. Even when the savings are more modest it is still a valuable exercise, and it gives you a great feeling of satisfaction, too.

There are new Internet-based ways of saving money, such as co-operative buying and price comparison sites (*Ideas 88* and *89*) to get you the best deal, as well as e-procurement (*Idea 90*) which is a great way for businesses to save money, or corporate bartering to ease your cash flow problems (*Idea 91*). Then there are all sorts of ways to find great deals online, such as those in *Ideas 92* and *93*. Or, if you're planning to move house, why not save up to a few thousand by selling your house yourself on the Net, instead of using an agent (*Idea 94*)?

Quite apart from the deals you can find on the Web, your line of communication itself gives you scope for saving money. The Internet Service Provider (ISP) you choose can make a difference to your wallet, too (*Idea 95*).

Once you get into the habit of checking the Net for new deals, you'll find there are plenty of opportunities to save money (such as the auctions and small ads we looked at in *Ideas 56* and *57*). Here are a few more ideas to help you get started.

Idea 88 – Shopping together

Everyone knows that if you buy in bulk you qualify for a discount. But you probably only need one washing machine or computer keyboard, so how can you get the benefit of bulk buying? Through co-operative buying, that's how.

Co-operative buying is a great use of the Internet to bring shoppers together to use their collective weight to bring prices down. The system is simple. The co-buying site lists all sorts of products that are available, and tells you what the retail price is, what the best possible price is, and the current price – which is determined by the number of buyers.

For example, if a particular washing machine costs £500 in the shops, it might be possible, with eight buyers or more, to bring the price down to, say, £380. The site also shows the current number of buyers and price, so that if five people have so far committed to buy, it indicates that the price is currently running at £405. It also tells you when the purchase closes, and you can choose whether you buy at whatever price it reaches, or only if it drops to a particular price.

Sites tend to offer a fairly wide range of goods at any one time, and some also allow you to suggest future products to buy. The sites all vary slightly, but they all operate on the same general principle. Check out the European www.letsbuyit.com, which asks you which country you are buying in, or the UK site www.adabra.com.

Idea 89 – Comparing notes

It has always been the case that if you spent long enough shopping around, you could generally get a better deal on most widely available items. Trouble is, we don't often have much time to traipse from shop to shop, or phone round them all. Luckily, we don't have to any more.

Price comparison sites utilise the ability to trawl the Web, and can find you the best deal on an item. They generally want your approximate location so they can take shipping costs into account as well. Then they show you a price comparison chart. Different sites offer different ranges of goods; www.dealpilot.com compares books, music and video products, whilst www.europe.streetprices.com is worth a look as it compares prices of a range of goods, and includes links to other price comparison sites.

Idea 90 – Buying time

The Net offers lots of ways for businesses to save money, as well as individuals. One of these is what is known as e-procurement; basically just business buying on the Net. One of the first and biggest businesses out there at the moment is Xaman.com. This organisation runs a Web site that enables customers to access catalogues and price lists of hundreds of suppliers, and place orders for furniture, computer supplies, even temporary staff. The site also enables buyers from overseas to place orders in their own currency, which the supplier will receive in sterling with any import duties and tax included.

Obviously having access to so many suppliers in one place makes it much easier to find the best prices, but the real saving is in the time it takes to do the buying. Xaman themselves claim that the costs of procurement can come down by a good 50 per cent.

Idea 91 – Fair exchange

Here's another idea for businesses. I'm not sure it's exactly saving money, but it certainly improves the money situation. Corporate bartering. Bartering of course is the practice of exchanging goods and services for each other, instead of trading them for cash. Or you can exchange them for 'barter pounds' or 'trading vouchers' or whatever the barter exchange you use deals in.

Corporate bartering is hugely popular in the US, used by over half of the top 500 fortune companies. The way it works is very simple. You offer goods and services to the pool of members, which they can purchase with credits that are credited to you. When you want goods and services yourself, you use these credits to acquire them from other members. Meanwhile the barter exchange company takes a commission. Invoices and purchase orders are raised as normal, put through your accounts, and you pay tax, including VAT, on the value just as you would if the deal had been done in hard currency.

Companies barter for all sorts of things, from consultancy to printing, restaurant covers to unsold stock. And why? Chiefly because it eases the pressure on their cash flow. Suppose you run a restaurant, and you need to spend £10,000 on printing, but you can't find the money in your budget. You simply barter for it instead, offering meals at your restaurant in exchange. Obviously the company that does your printing doesn't have to be the same one that takes the restaurant meals – it almost certainly won't be.

Corporate bartering has other advantages too. You no longer have to chase other organisations for bad debt, for a start. You're likely to make additional sales, and to build good long-term relationships with your customers. You can find corporate bartering organisations at www.barter.demon.co.uk and at www.tbex.com.

Ask yourself

What resources, goods or services do we have that we could barter to ease our cash flow?

Idea 92 – Deals on wheels

The debate is fierce about why cars are generally priced so much higher in the UK than they are in much of Europe, and UK car buyers resent having to pay such vastly inflated prices. Well, they don't have to any more.

The Internet has made it possible for UK consumers to buy cars at European prices, without even leaving the house. You can compare prices across Europe, and buy the customised model of your choice at up to 40 per cent less than UK forecourt prices. What's more, www.oneswoop.com will sort out warranties, insurance, finance options, registration, import regulations, tax and home delivery for you.

Cars are not the only product where buying in Europe is cheaper, but they are one of the most notorious, and oneswoop.com is a perfect example of how the Internet is making cost savings of several thousand pounds possible for all of us.

Idea 93 – Last minute buys

One of the most famously successful Internet businesses is lastminute.com. The idea behind this business was to offer really good deals on eleventh hour travel tickets, but they also do great deals on sport and concert tickets, events, hotel bookings, holidays and the like, and point you towards restaurants that have special offers running.

If you like to travel, take holidays, eat out or attend concerts, sporting fixtures or other events, you'll be able to save money through this Web site.

Idea 94 – Selling your own home

There are plenty of things we sell or buy through agents, giving them a cut along the way. Probably the most expensive of these are our houses. What does an estate agent charge – two per cent? Four per cent?

But it's getting easier and easier to sell online without agents, because it is so much simpler and cheaper to get in touch with potential buyers. And sites where you can sell your house, for a flat fee of under £100, are popping up. They may not be that big yet, but they're growing all the time. And think of the money you could save – thousands of pounds. Some sites also give advice on handling the legal aspects of the sale yourself, but of course you don't have to do this unless you want to. Still, it would save you even more …

Try www.ukhousehunter.co.uk and www.houseweb.co.uk if you want to check out house selling (and buying) on the Net.

Idea 95 – What's the whISPer?

One of the most basic of all ways to save money on the Internet is to use the most cost effective Internet Service Provider (ISP). It doesn't make sense to change ISP every week, but at the same time we often stick with what we've got even when it is no longer the best deal around.

In the old days (in the Internet time frame), you paid a subscription to your ISP and paid the cost of the phone calls on top. After a while, ISPs undercut this system by charging a subscription and then giving a set amount of time free of call charges. Or you could take out a free subscription and pay call charges only. Then there are the ISPs who offer a free subscription and free calls at off-peak times. And eventually – it had to happen – ISPs who are genuinely, totally free. No subscription charge and no phone charges.

How do they do this, you might wonder? They can make money out of advertising revenue, percentages of e-commerce transacted on certain sites, and data capture. And many of them have another agenda, too. For example, they may be trying to attract people to their long-distance call service, or some other paid phone service.

Never mind how they do it; the important point is that you really don't need to pay much – if anything – for your connection. For businesses it may be worth paying to ensure a high standard of service, but for home users there are plenty of ISPs that offer a perfectly satisfactory service completely free.

Ask yourself

What exactly am I paying in total for my Internet connection, and could I do better?

Five Greatest Ideas for Making Money for Charity

One of the great things about the boom in the Internet industry is that there's more than enough money to go around. So while you're on your way to making your first million, you can make sure others aren't missing out either.

The Internet has spawned all sorts of new ways of doing business for everyone, and that includes charities. If you work for a charity and want to raise money, *Ideas 96* and *97* will give your fundraising a boost. And if you simply want to help charities – without any cost to yourself – try *Ideas 98* to *100*. And don't let anyone tell you that the Internet isn't a good thing.

Idea 96 – Keep the bidding going

Successful charities have long known that auctions are a great way of raising money. If you don't want to hold a live auction, you can hold a silent one, where a list of bids is displayed and anyone who wants to can add a higher bid than the top one so far shown for any item. The highest bid at the designated closing time wins.

As you can imagine, this style of auction lends itself perfectly to the Internet. Of course, you still have to persuade your supporters to donate items for auction, and the more you promote the auction the more successful it will be. You can run an auction for anywhere between a week and a couple of months, to give bidders plenty of time.

You can run charity auctions via online auction sites, such as www.webcharity.com, or of course through a standard auction site such as eBay. The auction site will generally take a commission of between ten and twenty per cent; WEBcharity.com adds a ten per cent premium (or less for very high-value bids) to each winning bid.

Another option is to set up an auction site of your own. You can buy software from OpenSite Technologies or Easy Auction that will allow you to do this. While online charity auctions are likely to increase in the future, you may well gain a great deal of novelty value from running one now. So why wait?

Idea 97 – Grant us thy charity

Grant-making trusts are one of the biggest sources of finance for many charities. But persuading them to make the grant is a nightmare for many charities. First you have to find out which trusts and foundations are likely to make grants in your geographic area, or for the particular type of project in question. And then you have to submit the proposal in just the way they like it – once you've found out what that is.

So an online centre for grant-making foundations is a dream, and one that is about to come true. www.cybergrants.com is a Web site that helps you find the most promising sources of funding for your area and project, and then guides you through filling out an online form that will satisfy the foundation's requirements.

Of course, grant-making trusts are not known for their pioneering use of the Web, but things are likely to change over the next few years. For a start, CyberGrants.com is encouraging them on board by offering them a complete grants management system. And those that are ahead of the field, many of which are corporate foundations, are singing the praises of Internet grant-making.

One of these is the Bell Atlantic Foundation, the philanthropic arm of the US telecommunications corporation. Since the beginning of 2000, they now accept grant proposals online only. They find that, by guiding grant-seekers through their online proposal form, the quality of their grant proposals improves hugely, and they now accept twice the percentage of proposals that they used to.

Idea 98 – Give as you click

We all like the idea of giving to charity, and for those of us with limited finances – or even those of us who already give elsewhere – the idea of donating to charity without spending any money is a great one. All it takes is a modicum of effort, and sometimes not even that.

There is a growing choice of Web sites to visit if you want to benefit charities; some of them even let you choose which charity you help. One of these is iPledge (which you can find at www.atkinson.dnx.co.uk). If you shop at any of a dozen or so partners, a percentage of the money you spend is donated – by those partners – to charity. Simply visit the partners going via iPledge's home page. Partners include Amazon.co.uk, who give three per cent of all you spend to iPledge, and ten per cent of all featured books and CDs. What's more, you choose which charity you want to benefit.

A similar operation is run by iGive, but along slightly different lines. They have teamed up with over 200 shopping sites, so that any time a registered member of iGive clicks on a partner's ad within the iGive shopping mall, the advertiser donates a small amount of money to the registered member's charity of choice. If you spend money once you're in the store, a percentage of your payment is given back to iGive, who then pass 100 per cent of the money donated to the charity of your choice. You can help by visiting www.igive.com. You could try www.greatergood.com for another variation on the same theme.

Idea 99 – Surfing for charity

Here's yet another approach. Remember *Idea 54* – getting paid to surf the Net? An Internet company called Digital Donation run a very similar system, except that instead of paying you, the money goes to a charity of your choice. You download a program that displays a small advertisement banner, which sits on your desktop, and the advertisers pay Digital Donation for every hour you spend surfing. Find them at www.digitaldonation.com.

Idea 100 – The Hunger Site

This final idea is my favourite of all, and is commonly reckoned by its supporters to be as good an example of the positive power of the World Wide Web as you will find. The Hunger Site (at www.thehungersite.com) aims to use the Net to ease world hunger. It does this through sponsors who pay for a quarter of a cup of staple food every time someone clicks on the button on The Hunger Site's home page.

The money is passed on directly to the United Nations World Food Program, who take less than ten per cent of the donation for administration, and put all the rest directly into feeding starving people around the globe. (The Hunger Site itself takes no money at all.)

What happens when you visit The Hunger Site is that the home page displays a button for you to click (it will accept only one click per day from each visitor). When you click on it, you are thanked, and shown a list of that day's sponsors. If there are eight sponsors, that means you have just donated two cups of food. If there are ten, you have donated two and a half cups, and so on.

From the sponsors point of view, it is well worthwhile. Not only can you click through to their sites from the list of sponsors on the 'thank you' page, but the positive association they gain from being a sponsor does their image untold good. And The Hunger Site itself also does a great deal of good. Since it began in June 1999, it has steadily increased the number of donations to several million a month (that's way over 20 million cups of food each month). There are days when the number of donations in 24 hours tops 400,000. Many people make The Hunger Site their home page so they can click on it every day as soon as they go online.

Perhaps the best way to give you an indication of how regular visitors feel about The Hunger Site is to show you a selection from the letters the Web site has received, and which you can find more of when you visit it:

'There is so much hunger in the world. One person can only do so much, but people working together can move mountains.'

'My English is bad, but your idea is great, beautiful. Thanks for you, this homepage is one hope for the world.'

'This is probably the best use of the Internet ever. Thank you for doing such a wonderful thing.'

'Thank you for providing me with an opportunity to make at least a small contribution to those less fortunate than myself in a safe, private, and responsible manner.'

'Angels do exist.'

'This is the greatest use I have ever seen the Internet used for.'

'This is the true essence of a networked world.'

Index